Actions for Biodiversity in the UK: approaches in UK to implementing the Convention on Biological Diversity

Edited by:

David Hill   Jo Treweek

Tina Yates   Mike Pienkowski

Written by:

David Baldock –   *Institute for European Environmental Policy*
Vin Fleming –   *Scottish Natural Heritage*
David Hill –   *Ecoscope Applied Ecologists*
David Pape –   *Hampshire County Council*
Mike Pienkowski –   *Joint Nature Conservation Committee (now at*
                       Royal Society for the Protection of Birds)
Jo Treweek –   *Institute of Terrestrial Ecology*
Tina Yates –   *Institute of Terrestrial Ecology*

BRITISH
ECOLOGICAL
SOCIETY

1996
Published for
The British Ecological Society
by
Field Studies Council

Cover picture: A biologically rich mosaic of habitats resulting from the maintenance and re-establishment of traditional mixed farming in northwestern Islay, U.K. (*Photo: Roger Wardle, FWAG*).

CONTENTS

Foreword

This booklet differs in two main ways from its predecessors in the *Ecological Issues* series, but we hope that it will be no less valuable. First, previous numbers have focused on particular issues in applied ecology whilst the present one addresses a much wider topic: the national implementation of a global convention on the wide subject of the conservation of biological diversity.

Second, this booklet arose not as a workshop devoted to its production but as a one-day seminar attended by about 70 persons and held at the Institute of Terrestrial Ecology, Monks Wood on 6 September 1994. The seminar "Actions for Biodiversity in the UK" outlined the various initiatives which have been put in place to promote conservation of biodiversity in this country, and explored the potential role of ecologists in promoting effective biodiversity conservation measures. The reactions of the participants then led the editors to the conclusion that the material in the presentations would be of use to a wider audience. This may be even wider than the normal readership of these booklets, who we know include teachers and students as well as those engaged in more specialised ecological activities. A central feature of the Convention on Biological Diversity is that nature conservation should not be just a special land-use but should be integrated fully into the policies influencing all other land- and sea-uses. It is also something which must involve people at all levels of activity from local to international. The potential users of this booklet are thus very widespread and numerous!

Although the emphasis is on the UK, the problems of biodiversity loss in every country can be tackled effectively only if considered in the global context. We note also that the United Kingdom is one of the first states to produce a national action plan in response to the requirements of the Convention. We hope that a small introduction to this may be of interest and use to workers engaged on comparable tasks in other countries. This is not to say that we consider the UK plan to be perfect, as will be apparent from the contents. However, we hope that both the successes and the mistakes may provide useful information for our colleagues.

For the reasons given above, most of the chapters were originally written as conference presentations. We would like to thank Brian Davis for summing up the meeting, and John Sheail, Stuart Dobson and Mike Roberts for hospitality at ITE Monks Wood. Chapter 1 (drafted by Jo Treweek) incorporates *inter alia* ideas presented by Robert May in an introductory lecture. Chapter 6 (drafted by David Hill) developed the presentation by Mark Avery. Mike Pienkowski, who drafted Chapter 3, would like to acknowledge discussions and contributions from many colleagues, especially but not exclusively among the staff of JNCC, particularly Dr E M Bignal, Ms S Davies, Dr C A Galbraith, Dr D McCracken, Mrs M A Palmer,

Dr T M Reed, M L Tasker and Miss S E Wenlock. Vin Fleming thanks Professor M B Usher, A J Kerr and Dr C Sydes for helpful comments on the text of Chapter 4. Chapters 2 and 5 were drafted by David Baldock and David Pape, respectively. We would like to thank Dr D W H Walton, Chairman of BES Ecological Affairs Committee, for his comments on drafts. The views expressed are not necessarily those of the employers of the editors or authors.

Finally, we should note that international commitments and action plans are only as good as their implementation. If this booklet helps wider participation in this exercise, it will have fulfilled its purpose.

The Editors

1. INTRODUCTION: BIODIVERSITY – WHAT IT IS AND WHY IT SHOULD BE CONSERVED

1.1 Introduction

International concern about the loss and degradation of natural resources has grown. Unfortunately, however, there is a lack of accurate information about the rate, severity and extent of damage to the environment as a result of human activity. More importantly, soundly based policies and actions are required to halt and reverse this trend. Pressure for international action to tackle these problems came to a head in Rio de Janeiro at the United Nations Conference on Environment and Development (UNCED) in June 1992, when the Convention on Biological Diversity (hereinafter "the Convention") was signed by Heads of State and Governments. The content of the Convention is summarised in Appendix 1. The need to implement the Convention's international agreements and obligations (outlined in Chapter 2) makes it essential to establish how biodiversity should best be conserved. This in turn requires clarification of the term "biodiversity", and consideration of why it should be conserved and the methods available for measuring it (this chapter, Section 2). Some of the relevant international and national agreements relating to biodiversity conservation are then summarised (Chapter 2). The UK government, the countryside agencies, local authorities and voluntary conservation organisations have all put mechanisms in place for meeting the requirements of these (Chapters 3, 4, 5 and 6, respectively).

Barriers to the implementation of the Convention remain, however (Chapter 7). Ecologists have a major part to play in developing the scientific basis for further action. The research agenda should be set to fill the gaps which remain in our knowledge about how best to conserve biodiversity. To be effective, conservation action needs to involve all. Ecologists are needed to provide analyses and recommendations, but their work needs to be accessible. This booklet is intended as one contribution towards this.

1.2 Biodiversity: what it is and where?

The term "biodiversity" has been given various definitions. The Convention's definition (Box 1.1) makes it clear that Biological Diversity does not mean simply "numbers of species". It is a concept which applies at all levels, from landscapes and ecosystems down to individual species and their gene pools. Variation at many scales of genetic, geographic and taxonomic expression must be taken into account. Current actions in Britain have tended to focus on species (and only a relatively

1

restricted range of these) as "units of conservation". The importance of preserving biological diversity at the genetic level has been neglected, "replacement" habitat (for example the seeding of wildflowers on roadside verges) often being established using seed or stock from other regions, or even countries. This has potentially damaged a heritage of richly textured local geographic variation. In the US, by contrast, recognition of the fact that species are embedded in a matrix of physical and biological interactions has resulted in conservation legislation being increasingly oriented towards ecosystems, not only to individual species. It is important that measures to conserve biodiversity should encompass variety at all relevant scales.

Internationally, the recording of biological diversity has been very uneven across the range of genera, families, orders of phyla and species. The marine realm, for example has been greatly under-represented. Roughly 1.7 or 1.8 million species have been named and recorded in total. However, this figure may need downward revision to take account of documented rates of synonymy (a single species being described as two or more) of about 20%, so that the total number of distinct species should perhaps be more like 1.4 million. The great majority of these species (about a million) are insects. Approximately a quarter of a million are flowering plants. Only 40-50,000 are vertebrates, birds numbering 9-10,000 and mammals about 4,000. Despite the fact that birds and mammals are less numerous than other groups, they have been studied much more thoroughly. In terms of biodiversity conservation, current research effort and expenditure is skewed towards the more "charismatic mega-vertebrates", some other groups and species being almost completely neglected. This is reflected in the scientific literature, with approximately one paper per species being published annually for birds and mammals, as compared to approximately 10% of a paper per species for invertebrates. Some of this bias

---

Box 1.1   The Convention's definition of Biological Diversity

"The variability among living organisms from all sources including, *inter alia*, terrestrial, marine and other aquatic ecosystems and the ecological complexes of which they are part; this includes diversity within species, between species and of ecosystems".

This definition recognises three levels of biodiversity:

a) Diversity between and within ecosystems and habitats;

b) Diversity of species;

c) Genetic variation within individual species;

all of which constitute what might be regarded as the "variety of life".

results from the interest of volunteers – who supply most of the basic information. Also relevant is the level of wider public interest and consequently legislation and information needed to fulfil its needs.

1.3   Patterns of endemism and endangerment

Some parts of the world are more richly endowed with species than others. Such rich areas are obviously important – but it is also important to maintain those areas which are naturally lower in species-number. Otherwise, those species of areas such as the arctic, mountains and some marine systems would be degraded. As is clear in Box 1, the purpose is to conserve the range of ecosystems and the species each supports, not simply to achieve the maximum number of species in all areas or to focus only on the naturally richest areas.

Whilst an objective is to conserve the full range of biodiversity, it is also an aim to maintain characteristic or representative ranges of habitats and species. The first logical step is to determine the distributions of organisms. The next is to identify how and where they are threatened. However, variable levels of survey/knowledge mean that it is difficult to establish with any accuracy both the extent to which many species are limited to only one region (endemism) and their patterns of endangerment.

It is worth noting that Britain has a better knowledge of some of the less charismatic species, compared with some other countries. Nevertheless, whilst butterflies attract the interest of amateurs or voluntary bodies, less appealing organisms like nematodes are still very neglected. Patterns of knowledge vary between groups, so knowledge of patterns of endangerment throughout the world is generally a "best guess". Based on criteria of IUCN (the World Conservation Union), on a global basis, something like a tenth of all bird and mammal species are endangered, and we have lost about 1% of them in the last couple of hundred years. This represents a rate of certified extinction which is about 10,000 times the background levels suggested by the fossil record, and official extinction rates are likely to be an under-estimate. For other vertebrates, the fact that there is a lower proportion of endangered categories is more likely to reflect less knowledge than less endangerment. Probably the most endangered single group of vertebrates are freshwater fish.

Of the total number of species known and recorded, the UK proportion varies from group to group (Box 1.2). Britain has a reasonable proportion of known biodiversity at the microbial level (which may reflect real differences in the geographical distribution of micro- versus larger organisms). Britain is also relatively rich in bryophytes and lichens, but poor in reptiles and amphibians. Excluding micro-organisms, about 3% of the world's recorded total of plant and animal species occur in Britain. In terms of global endangerment, Britain might be considered to be in relatively good shape, perhaps because it has already lost many species or because it was never very rich in the first place.

Box 1.2	Terrestrial and freshwater species in the UK, compared with estimated global totals		
Group	**Global total species**	**UK total species**	**UK as % of global**
Protozoa	40,000?	20,000	50?
Algae	40,000?	20,000	50?
Fungi	70,000	12,000	17
Ferns	12,000	80	0.7
Bryophytes	14,000	1,000	7.0
Lichens	17,000	1,500	9.0
Flowering plants	270,000	1,400	0.5
Insects	1,000,000	22,500	2
Other invertebrates	300,000?	6,000	2
Freshwater fish	8,500?	~40	0.5
Reptiles & amphibians	10,500	12	0.1
Mammals	4,000	48	1.2
Birds	9,500	210	2
TOTAL	**1,800,000**	**88,000**	**5**

1.4   Reasons for conserving biodiversity

Why should biodiversity be conserved? Taking a utilitarian approach, there are three main reasons why the conservation of biodiversity has been considered important enough to warrant concerted international action.

The first is based on the view that the diversity of species may form the basis for new foods, chemicals and pharmaceuticals. There is a strong economic argument for conserving resources which may have potential value for future industrial exploitation. Second, conservation of biological diversity has also been promoted for reasons of precaution or "insurance". Biological systems have created and maintained the biosphere as an oxygen-rich place in which increasingly complicated life flourishes. As it is unclear how diverse a system needs to be in order to maintain its function, any loss of component parts is a potential threat to its viability. The degree of human dependence on existing ecosystems is only partially understood. It is possible that we could operate in a world vastly simpler than the one we live in and that we might be clever enough to do it. Even if this were possible (which is far from accepted), the question is whether we would want to.

The most important and enduring utilitarian argument for the conservation of biological diversity is also an ethical one which rests on the "imperative of stewardship" and the obligation to hand on to future human generations a world which has not become significantly or irreversibly impoverished. As Mrs Margaret Thatcher, then the British Prime Minister, said, "we do not have a freehold on the planet; we have a full repairing lease".

Other reasons include the appreciation of people for "natural beauty". The "variety of life" forms an integral part of people's perceptions of their environment, and may have a vital part to play in the maintenance of a sense of spiritual well-being.

The utilitarian arguments outlined above have been instrumental in promoting biodiversity conservation internationally. However, there are a number of difficulties which arise from approaches grounded solely in a utilitarian philosophy. Perceptions of the meaning and importance of biodiversity conservation can vary according to the spatial scale at which individuals interact with their environment. For the great majority of people, local issues take priority because of direct influences on the use and enjoyment of immediate surroundings. Often, however, the significance of biodiversity loss is greater at higher spatial scales and affects areas which tend to be less intensively inhabited (for example coral reefs, wetland biosphere reserves and so on). The allocation of resources for biodiversity conservation tends to reflect this tendency, often resulting in the neglect of key areas.

1.5   International legislation to tackle biodiversity loss

These arguments for the conservation of biodiversity have now been accepted by governments across the world, at the "Earth Summit" (UN Conference on the Environment and Development – UNCED), held in Rio de Janeiro, Brazil in June 1992. The background to this conference is outlined in Chapter 2, which notes the range of agreements reached as well as the approaches the Member States of the European Union have taken to these commitments.

The Member States agreed to prepare summary progress reports for the national strategies. In January 1994 the UK Government published four strategic documents in partial fulfilment of the commitments made at the Rio Earth Summit. These were: *Sustainable Development: the UK Strategy (Cm. 2426)*; *Climate Change: the UK Programme (Cm. 2427)*; *Biodiversity: the UK Action Plan (Cm. 2428)* and *Sustainable Forestry: the UK Programme (Cm. 2429)*. At the same time, new institutional structures were announced to take these documents forward. Chapter 3 sets the UK Government's Biodiversity Action Plan in a context of cross-sectoral approaches to conservation and some future needs.

Throughout a consideration of the needs to fulfil the Convention, it is important to bear in mind that it is not enough just to maintain the status quo. Whilst it is important to ensure that existing distributions of native species in their natural ranges are maintained, in many of the more developed countries, like the UK, the status quo may actually be an already highly degraded state. Accordingly, the need for restoration is clear both in the preamble to the Convention and in Article 8. It is necessary to set positive targets for restoration of a range of species. For these to be

---

Box 1.3   Summary of chapter contents

Chapter 1 notes the rapid loss of biodiversity due to human action and reasons for conserving biodiversity. These arguments have been accepted by governments across the world, resulting in the Convention. Ecologists have a role not just in providing some of the information needs but in making these accessible to the wide range of people who need to be aware of, and active in, these issues.

Chapter 2 outlines the historical and political background to the Rio Conference and the range of international agreements which resulted from it. The approaches taken by the Member States of the European Union to implementing the Convention on Biological Diversity are then discussed.

Chapter 3 notes the main requirements of the Convention on Biological Diversity, highlighting the central need to incorporate conservation into other human activities. The UK Government's production of a national biodiversity action plan is outlined, with its important involvement of non-governmental organisations and its joint sponsorship by all government departments. The further need to develop assessable, timed targets relating to cross-sectoral policies is noted. Some examples of how planning authorities and industry have taken account of nature conservation interest in widescale and cross-sectoral planning operations are summarised. Some further work requirements are indicated, focusing on the objective of maintaining and restoring the regional diversity of the heritage. This needs work on relating the requirements of regionally characteristic wildlife to the effects of land-use, especially agricultural, policies and practices.

Box 1.3   Summary of chapter contents (cont'd)

Chapter 4 outlines the fundamental role of the statutory country nature conservation agencies in contributing to the achievement of the objectives of *Biodiversity: the UK Action Plan*. It is clear that the achievement of these targets cannot depend on agency efforts alone but will rely upon their ability to work with, persuade and encourage others to work to common goals. Key participants in this respect will be other parts of national and local government, researchers, voluntary bodies, local planning authorities, land managers and the general public. This chapter outlines the role of the country agencies in achieving the Plan objectives, taking examples mainly from the work of Scottish Natural Heritage. The contribution of traditional work and new initiatives to the attainment of targets, and the research required to underpin these, are reviewed with reference to specific examples.

Chapter 5 focuses on the role of local authorities in conserving biodiversity. The main emphasis is on the conservation of habitats and species through forward planning and control of development. The most recent thinking on evaluation systems and development plan policies to help conserve the biological resource is reviewed, taking examples mainly from the experience of Hampshire County Council. The approach is specifically tailored to meeting sustainable development objectives. The concept of critical natural capital (irreplaceable resource) is a useful basis for identifying the most important areas beyond statutory sites. All critical natural capital deserves particularly strong protection in development plans. To maintain biodiversity, it is important also to strive for no net loss of natural assets. In addition to the safeguard of critical natural capital, it is therefore essential to give appropriate protection to the rest of the nature conservation resource and to secure replacement where loss or damage occurs.

Chapter 6 summarises the approach of a consortium of UK voluntary nature conservation societies. Its thrust is that planning and action to conserve UK biodiversity should be sharply focused on outcome, i.e. what needs to be achieved for individual species in terms of numbers and ranges, and habitats in terms of extent and quality. The document provides broad conservation objectives and detailed targets for species and habitats in the UK, with over 600 species targets and 35 habitat targets identified for action over the next 10 years. Conservation action plans should be written as soon as possible for all priority species and habitats. To be successful, conservation objectives and targets must be embedded in all aspects of government policy and action, as the conservation of biodiversity is a key test of sustainability. A wide range of threats face the natural environment – calling for an equally wide range of solutions, involving much improved research and monitoring as well as policy shifts in areas such as agriculture, fisheries and forestry. By addressing the resources needed for biodiversity conservation and considering the various approaches to costing biodiversity targets, conservation action can often make more economic sense and sometimes be cheaper than implementing schemes which damage the environment.

Chapter 7 looks to some of the needs for further work to achieve the commitments in UK under the Convention on Biological Diversity.

realistic, some assessment of potential is necessary. This is explored in Chapter 3. To fulfil these needs, Chapters 4, 5 and 6 centre on the roles of statutory conservation agencies, local authorities and non-governmental organisations.

2. THE EUROPEAN PERSPECTIVE AFTER UNCED – OBLIGATIONS FOR EUROPEAN GOVERNMENTS

2.1 Background

The United Nations' Conference on Environment and Development, was the largest high-level conference on the environment ever. The 150 countries represented (most by their heads of government) agreed five important documents (Box 2.1), and the theme of Sustainable Development was elevated to the mainstream of international relations.

UNCED was timed to take place 20 years after the first UN Conference on the Environment in Stockholm in 1972. Its origins can be traced to the report of the World Commission on Environment and Development chaired by Mrs Brundtland, the former Norwegian Prime Minister, which was published by the UN in 1987. This document first gave currency to the phrase "sustainable development" and helped to build support for a global conference. Two years later, at the UN General Assembly in 1989, a formal resolution was passed calling for a summit to take place (Resolution 44/228).

While environment and development were central themes at UNCED, the event must be seen in the context of the continuing debate between Northern and Southern governments about trade, aid and the control of resources. Some of the fiercest debates during the conference were concerned with the extent of aid which Northern governments were prepared to offer the South in return for sharing new environmental obligations. The US government prevaricated over whether to sign the Biodiversity Convention, partly because of apparent fears over the costs of implementing the Convention, and the prospect that Southern governments might acquire greater control over genetic resources.

Box 2.1 The two new conventions and three other documents agreed at UNCED

- the Rio Declaration on Environment and Development

- Agenda 21, an Action Plan for the Next Century

- the Convention on Biological Diversity

- the Framework Convention on Climate Change

- a Statement of Principles for Sustainable Management of Forests

---

2.2   The Agreements

The Rio Declaration is the shortest of the documents agreed at UNCED, consisting of a list of 27 Principles. These are an attempt to encapsulate some of the main themes of the sustainable development debate and the broader North/South agenda accompanying it. The rights of different parties are given due emphasis – human rights in Principle 1, the rights of women in Principle 20 and government rights in Principle 2. Some of the most important Principles pertaining particularly to the environment are nos 3, 4 and 7. The text of these follows:

Principle 3 – The right to development must be fulfilled so as to equitably meet developmental and environmental needs of present and future generations.

Principle 4 – In order to achieve sustainable development, environmental protection shall constitute an integral part of the development process and cannot be considered in isolation from it.

Principle 7 – States shall cooperate in a spirit of global partnership to conserve, protect and restore the health and integrity of the Earth's ecosystems. In view of the different contributions to global environmental degradation, States have common but differentiated responsibilities. The developed countries acknowledge the responsibility that they bear in the international pursuit of sustainable development in view of the pressures their societies place on the global environment and of the technologies and financial resources they command.

The basic principles of the Rio Declaration form a prelude to Agenda 21. This, by contrast, is a voluminous document of some 800 pages, attempting to set out an international agenda for the 21st century. Perhaps the most important aims are to achieve:

* Sustainable development on a global scale;

* A move towards a global consensus on the way forward;

* An emphasis on the role of national governments as the main actors;

* The establishment of a new institution, the UN Commission for Sustainable Development (CSD), to take the initiative forward. (This met for the first time in June 1993 in New York City.)

Among the many chapters of Agenda 21 is one concerned with biodiversity. This proposes a basis for action, a set of objectives and a series of potential activities, some related to the management of resources, others to the collection of data and information, and a further group to international and regional co-operation. In a discussion of the means for implementation, a budget of US $3.5 billion per annum for the years 1993-2000 is suggested, perhaps half in the form of grants or finance on concessional terms.

The Convention on Biological Diversity was signed in Rio by the European Community, as well as by national governments. The text was based on a draft prepared originally by the UN Environment Programme Secretariat and developed during the course of meetings stretching from 1991 onwards. The objectives of the Convention are:

- The conservation of biological diversity;

- The sustainable use of its components;

- The fair and equitable sharing of the benefits arising from the utilisation of genetic resources.

The text itself contains 42 articles and places a sizeable number of obligations on signatories, many of them of a rather general nature. (However, some are addressed in more detail in other international conventions, to which the Biodiversity Convention can be considered as an "umbrella" agreement.) One of the most important obligations is to develop, or adapt, existing national strategies, plans or programmes for the conservation and sustainable use of biological diversity. Signatories are also obliged, as far as is possible and appropriate, to integrate the conservation and sustainable use of biological diversity into relevant sectoral or cross-sectoral plans, programmes and policies. Other obligations cover in-situ and ex-situ conservation, the identification and monitoring of biodiversity, research and training, the use of incentives for conservation, environmental impact assessment, access to genetic resources and technology, technical and scientific co-operation and financial resources. One of the requirements for in-situ conservation is that Contracting Parties should, as far as is possible and appropriate, establish a system of protected areas or areas where special measures need to be taken to conserve biological diversity. The coverage of the most relevant Articles is summarised in Appendix 1.

In order to assist developing countries in implementing the Convention, there is provision for financial assistance, initially through the Global Environment Facility, and possibly later by a new institution.

Developing countries should be compensated for extraction of their genetic material, while developed countries should regulate the activities of biotechnology firms.

The Framework Convention on Climate Change also was signed by both the European Community and Member States. The main objective is to stabilise greenhouse gas concentrations in the atmosphere at a level which will prevent dangerous anthropogenic changes in the world's climate. The principal obligation on Contracting Parties is to prepare and publish national inventories of emissions of greenhouse gases and national (or regional) programmes of action on emissions and sinks. The stabilisation of emissions at 1990 levels by the year 2000 is stated as a desirable aim for developed countries but it is not a formal obligation for signatories of the Convention. This has obvious linkages to the conservation of biological diversity, but is not considered further in this booklet.

The fifth and final document to emerge from Rio was the Statement of Forest Principles. More formally, this is known as the "Non-legally binding authoritative statement of principles for a global consensus on the management, conservation and sustainable development of all types of forests". Many European countries argued that this agreement should have the status of an international convention but they failed to achieve a consensus on this point. Many developing countries, for example, remained suspicious that they would be required to give undertakings for the conservation of their own forests before they were ready to do so – and without adequate reciprocal action or financial support by the richer Northern countries. Consequently, the Statement is not legally binding. The Principles are intended to express a global consensus on the management, conservation and sustainable development of all types of forest. Shortly after the Forest Principles were signed, the EC and G-7 countries agreed an eight point plan for follow-up action, including a commitment to publish national plans showing how they intend to implement the Principles.

Since Rio, there has been some progress towards following up the various agreements. The new Commission for Sustainable Development has come into operation and has a secretariat based in New York. Two sessions of the Commission had been held by autumn 1994.

2.3   European action

In the aftermath of Rio, European Community governments reached agreement on an eight-point plan for follow-up to UNCED (Box 2.2).

In June 1993 the European Council reaffirmed their commitment to this eight-point plan and agreed on a programme of action. Amongst the commitments in this programme was one stressing that the Community and Member States should play an active role in the work of the Intergovernmental Committee for the Convention on Biological Diversity so as to secure the best possible preparation of the first session of the Conference of the Parties, which subsequently took place in 1994.

Within the European Community the principal document setting out the strategy for implementing the objectives of *Agenda 21* is the fifth Environmental Action Programme. Although this was drawn up prior to the Rio Conference, it picks up many of the same themes and is entitled *Towards Sustainability*. The programme covers the years 1992-2000 and is due to be reviewed and probably amended by the end of 1995. It has an emphasis on integrating environmental considerations into

---

Box 2.2   The aims of the EC plan to follow-up UNCED

- ratify the Climate Change Convention and publish national implementation plans
- publish plans for action on biodiversity and establish the basis for ratification of the Convention
- publish national plans for implementing the Forestry Principles
- publish national plans for the implementation of the Rio Declaration and *Agenda 21*
- support developing countries in implementing *Agenda 21* through development assistance and replenishment of the Global Environment Facility (GEF)
- take the lead in establishing a Sustainable Development Commission
- put weight behind establishing an international review process for the Forestry Principles
- take the lead in the restructuring of the GEF so that it can become the permanent financial mechanism for the Biodiversity and Climate Change Conventions

---

other Community policies, including industry, energy, transport, agriculture and tourism. It is not binding on the Community or its Member States but it does propose action to be taken at Community level, at national level and by local authorities.

Both the Community and individual Member States have a role in fulfilling the obligations of the Climate Change and Biodiversity Conventions. The Community ratified both Conventions in December 1993, although many Member States were not able to adhere to this timetable. The great majority of Member States had ratified the Climate Convention by mid 1994.

Whereas the Climate Convention has been associated with major legislative proposals and political debate within the EC, there has been less discussion at Community level about implementation of the Biodiversity Convention. Although legal competence for fulfilling the obligations of the Convention are divided between the Community and its Member States, it is clear that the main Community initiative in this area is the Habitats and Species Directive 92/43, as well as the earlier Birds Directive 79/409 and Directives on Environmental Impacts and Environmental Information. The Habitats Directive was agreed at about the same time as the Rio Conference in 1992 and will come into effect over the period up to 2004. At present, there are no plans for other major EC initiatives in this sphere. The Community will develop an EC response for the conservation of biological diversity; but much of this task will fall to individual Member States. Additionally, it should be noted that the Council of Europe is leading an initiative to prepare an outline of a European Biological and Landscape Diversity Strategy. Clearly, if

13

adopted, such a strategy would have a different status to one prepared by the EC and would cover a larger group of countries.

The Community participated in the Helsinki Conference on the protection of forests in Europe in 1993. There are no plans for a major initiative to implement the Helsinki guidelines at Community level although the mechanisms for subsidising afforestation and forestry management were strengthened in 1992 (Regulation 2080/92). At an international level, the EC has been involved in a large pilot project on tropical forests in Brazil, and the EC policy on tropical forests is being developed. The Community has stated on several occasions its commitment to a future legally binding global Forest Convention, which would become a successor to the current Forest Principles. In the short term, Member States have agreed to produce full national plans and "comprehensive reports" for the implementation of the Forest Principles, including summaries in an agreed common format.

Individual Member States have moved at varying speeds to respond to the agreements made at Rio. The UK was the first to produce a suite of four national reports, launched at the same time by the Prime Minister and other Ministers on 25 January 1994. The contents of *Biodiversity: the UK Action Plan* are discussed in the next Chapter.

3.   UK RESPONSIBILITIES UNDER THE CONVENTION ON BIOLOGICAL DIVERSITY

3.1   Requirements of the Convention

The Convention on Biological Diversity was agreed on 5 June 1992 in Rio de Janeiro, and came into force in late 1993. It was ratified by the United Kingdom in June 1994.

Article 1 of the Convention on Biological Diversity sets out the objectives, which include: "the conservation of biological diversity, the sustainable use of its components and the fair and equitable sharing of the benefits arising".

Nature conservation is primarily concerned with maintaining natural biodiversity. The Convention underlines this in its preamble: "noting ... that the fundamental requirement for the conservation of biological diversity is the in-situ conservation of ecosystems and natural habitats and the maintenance and recovery of viable populations of species in their natural surroundings." This should not be confused with increasing the number of species, whether natural or not, in an area.

The Convention (see definitions in Box 1.1) is not concerned just with rare species or protected sites. It is equally important to maintain ranges of populations by policies relevant throughout the countryside, both to prevent species' becoming rare and to ensure that wildlife can be experienced by the public.

The Convention is concerned also with "sustainable use", defined as "the use of components of biological diversity in a way and at a rate that does not lead to the long-term decline of biological diversity, thereby maintaining its potential to meet the needs and aspirations of present and future generations". Using this definition, it is clear that, whereas some of the traditional ways in which people use tropical forests are relatively sustainable, some of the modern commercial timber extraction methods, which disrupt forest ecosystems and reduce ranges of wildlife and native people, are not sustainable. Similarly, low-intensity agricultural systems – working within local environmental constraints – tend to be sustainable. In parts of Europe, the long period of continuity between humans and their environment also contributes particularly to biodiversity. There are other good examples in coastal systems, which are receiving attention as engineers increasingly recognise the value of natural processes in coastal defence. Nevertheless, in such cases, there may well be ways of introducing relevant modern techniques to assist and improve systems based on traditional practices. Article 10 requires that traditional cultures should be supported in practices compatible with sustainable use and to implement remedial action in degraded areas.

Box 3.1   The goal, principles and objectives of the UK Biodiversity Action Plan

Overall goal
To conserve and and enhance biological diversity within the UK and to contribute to the conservation of global diversity through all appropriate mechanisms.

Underlying principles
1.   Where biological resources are used, such use should be sustainable.
2.   Wise use should be ensured for non-renewable resources.
3.   The conservation of biodiversity requires the care and involvement of individuals and communities as well as Governmental processes.
4.   Conservation of biodiversity should be an integral part of Government programmes, policy and action.
5.   Conservation practice and policy should be based upon a sound knowledge base.
6.   The precautionary principle should guide decisions.

Objectives for conserving biodiversity
1.   To conserve and where practicable to enhance:
   a) the overall populations and natural ranges of native species and the quality and range of wildlife habitats and ecosystems;
   b) internationally important and threatened species, habitats and ecosystems;
   c) species, habitats and natural and managed ecosystems that are characteristics of local areas;
   d) the biodiversity of natural and semi-natural habitats where this has been diminished over recent past decades.

2.   To increase public awareness of, and involvement in, conservation biodiversity.

3.   To contribute to the conservation of biodiversity on a European and global scale.

Objectives for nature conservation should be considered across the entire countryside, as special sites alone are unlikely to sustain viable populations in the long-term. Neither will wildlife restricted to protected sites be accessible to most people. Protection of elite sites will remain one of the key mechanisms contributing to conservation policies but it must be considered only one of a suite of mechanisms. This need to influence cross-sectoral policies (i.e. policies relating to other human activities, such as agriculture and transport) is also at the heart of the Convention on Biological Diversity (as well as being necessary to fulfil requirements under EC Directives such as 79/409 on the Conservation of Wild Birds, and other international commitments such as the "Ramsar" Convention on Wetlands of International Importance).

Article 6 of the Convention requires each Contracting Party to:

"(a) develop national strategies, plans or programmes for the conservation and sustainable use of biological diversity ... and

(b) integrate, as far as possible and as appropriate, the conservation and sustainable use of biological diversity into relevant sectoral or cross-sectoral plans, programmes and policies."

Article 8(c) underlines the wide-ranging application of this requirement by requiring Contracting Parties to "regulate or manage biological resources important for the conservation of biological diversity whether within or outside protected areas, with a view to ensuring their conservation and sustainable use".

3.2 The United Kingdom Government's approach: the UK Biodiversity Action Plan

Even before ratifying the Convention in 1994, the United Kingdom government committed itself to produce a national action plan under the Convention by the end of 1993. The government's *Biodiversity: The UK Action Plan* was prepared on the basis of wide consultations with interested parties, and was agreed across government departments.

The preparation of this plan broke new ground. The Government invited a range of individuals from government departments, agencies and non-governmental organisations to draft the various chapters. As the final document was a statement by Government, these drafts were subject to later rewriting within the core of the government machine.

The different perceptions of governmental and non-governmental participants were interesting. The traditional British governmental approach to its international commitments has been described as producing an account of existing or previous work to prove that the UK has already done everything necessary. This could account for the very descriptive nature of the text. However, major progress has been achieved with the incorporation of clear objectives and progress towards these (Boxes 3.1 & 3.2).

A further criticism by conservationists was that the Action Plan contained nothing new. In contrast, during the preparation, officials of government departments frequently expressed concern that some drafting might imply new governmental commitments. A good deal of mutual education is clearly required. However, whilst conservationists may consider that the plan does not go far enough, a major step forward is that the plan is issued by the full range of government departments and not just those with the lead on environmental matters.

In such a complex collaborative process, it proved impracticable to develop precise targets in the time available, but the published stage did record 59 items as "Progress towards objectives."

Although Government requires its agencies to provide plans specifying assessable targets with a clear timescale, Government itself found this rather challenging. Forty-two of the 59 items noted above relate to habitats and species, via policies directed to site-management, direct species-conservation or to other economic sectors. Box 3.2 summarises the 42 on this basis. (The others of the 59 concern

---

Box 3.2   The nature of the item listed under "Progress towards objectives" in the UK Biodiversity Action Plan

Nature of "progress" item	Site-based	Species-based	Cross-sectoral	Total
Readily assessable, with timescale	3	2	1	6
Readily assessable, without timescale	4	2	3	9
Not readily assessable	3	1	23	27

---

development of public awareness and contributions to international conservation.) Overall, the lack of assessable targets is striking, and Government committed itself to produce such targets by the European Year of Nature Conservation 1995. There was evident difficulty in agreeing assessable targets for the cross-sectoral issues, which lie at the heart of the Convention, compared with site-based or species-focused matters.

To demonstrate the feasibility of a more specific approach, a consortium of voluntary conservation bodies put forward over 530 species targets and 16 habitat targets. Whilst this *Biodiversity Challenge* (see Chapter 6) goes a long way towards identifying and justifying specific targets at the more threatened end of the scale, further work is needed to develop an approach which prevents species becoming rare in the first place. In addition, some have suggested that the large number of targets should be integrated into a smaller number more easily assimilated by the public and politicians.

The challenge for both governmental bodies and non-statutory organisations is to identify objectives and targets relevant for both rare and common species, and to relate these to human operations in the countryside, especially agriculture, forestry and fisheries. This is central to an integration of nature conservation into other land- and sea-uses.

3.3 Needs to fulfil the Convention's requirements

In the early aftermath of the signing of the Convention, several staff of the Joint Nature Conservation Committee (JNCC – the Government's statutory adviser on national and international nature conservation) attempted to identify the work needed to fulfil the Convention's requirements. The summary diagram is reprinted as Box 3.3. As discussed above, the development of the UK's plan did not follow such a pattern, but we can examine the main balance of current and previous effort and future requirements.

The upper left part of the diagram seems to have progressed rather further than the right side. Whilst considerable surveys of certain taxa remain lacking, major progress has been made in many areas. Database-linking has a long way to go but some steps are being taken along a usefully modular path. Due to the profitable partnership of professional and amateur workers, the UK benefits from some of the best time-series monitoring of wildlife anywhere in the world. Work is needed to develop this for more taxa and to improve links with the results of monitoring land-use.

On the right side, work has started on a range of targeting systems. The preamble to the Convention on Biological Diversity emphasises that a basic series of targets is required to prevent further declines in native species. However, maintenance of the *status quo* is not, by itself, enough. This is because of the drastic losses of wildlife suffered in recent years. The Convention requires each Contracting Party to "rehabilitate and restore degraded ecosystems" (Article 8f).

Work on collating requirements for the maintenance of wildlife and its sustainable use, assessing threats and opportunities, and developing land-use management recommendations is minimal. There are, however, good examples in the UK of other land- and sea-users and regulatory authorities being prepared to take account

Box 3.3.   A framework to achieve the conservation of biological diversity to fulfil relevant Articles of the Convention. This (from Pienkowski 1993) develops an earlier model designed to encourage a move from simply reporting changes in the wildlife resource towards setting positive targets against which to assess our stewardship of wildlife populations. (The flow starts at the top left, but recycles through this area.)

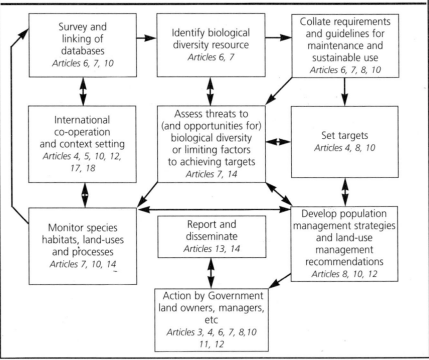

of nature conservation interests over wide areas provided that information can be provided at a suitably non-technical level, but supported by sound data as necessary.

3.4   Some examples of effective nature conservation science input to cross-sectoral plans and policies

Regional Indicative Forest Strategies

The UK has a relatively low proportion of land under forest, and current policies favour substantial increase. However, the major increase has been by planting extensive areas of even-age North American coniferous trees in upland areas, rather than by re-establishment of native-species woodlands in upland and lowland areas. This has a major impact on the natural and semi-natural populations of characteristic plants and animals and ecosystem processes. There are also considerable impacts on other aspects of the environment and the local communities. Accordingly, Regional Councils in Scotland each prepared an indicative strategy showing areas where there should be a presumption in favour of, or against, afforestation (subject to local considerations), taking account of these various interests and impacts.

Initially, there was no mechanism to take account of nature conservation factors alongside other interests. However, conservation scientists noted that these strategies could potentially assist in fulfilling the UK's commitments under EC Directive 79/409 on the Conservation of Wild Birds. This requires Member States to take special measures to conserve certain bird species. Some of these species are dependent on extensive areas, and site-safeguard measures alone are inadequate to provide suitable conservation.

Fortunately, data on birds gathered largely by volunteers in Britain and elsewhere in Europe were available to provide the necessary sound basis on which to provide nature conservation advice. Work is in hand to extend the process to other aspects of nature conservation interest, where appropriate and feasible, for future revisions of the strategy.

The occurrence of species sensitive to large-scale afforestation were assembled on a 10x10 km grid, to avoid publication of locations which could have put these birds at risk. The importance of each 10 x 10 km square for each species was assessed by comparing (with the relevant UK population) the number of individuals or pairs supported. The scores for those species which would be adversely affected by the development were then summed to give an overall score for each square. The squares in each region were then grouped into high, medium and low interest.

Regional planners indicated that they found this simplified assessment extremely helpful. This was demonstrated by a substantial change to the earliest draft strategy to take account of this information on nature conservation. Input to strategies for other Regions was made at an earlier stage, so that the impact on the strategies is likely to have been at least as great. This work is an important step in developing a strategic assessment of the upland bird resource, and linking it to major land uses in an international context.

Offshore oil exploration and development

The discovery of oil and gas under the North Sea gave rise to concerns on the part of conservationists that subsequent exploration could endanger the natural environment, particularly seabirds, as substantial proportions of the world populations of several species depend on the seas off north-western Europe.

In the 1970s, almost nothing was known of the spatial and seasonal distribution of these birds in their feeding habitat, the sea. Accordingly, a consortium was formed by the oil industry, related government departments and the Nature Conservancy Council (then the Government's nature conservation agency) to investigate this.

The JNCC's (formerly NCC's) Seabirds at Sea Team has now surveyed the seas around most of Britain to provide an effort-corrected index of occurrence of each species in each "statistical rectangle" covering 15' N-S x 30' E-W (at these latitudes, approximately 25 km x 25 km). In order to make the information easily usable by the industry, a single vulnerability map was produced for each month of the year. This combined information on the sensitivity of each species to surface pollution with the importance of each area to that species, finally integrating the results for all species to produce the summary users' maps. The work has now been developed to integrate more recent work from co-workers in other European countries to refine the vulnerability index.

These results and supporting information have been used by government in determining which areas to license for exploration and what conditions to place on activities, especially in relation to seasons of operation. The industry uses the information in preparing its proposals and plans. There is also some use developing in the oil-transport industry, and this would benefit from much further progress.

Agricultural land-use and nature conservation

The preceding two examples relate essentially to the limiting of potentially negative effects on wildlife, by strategic targeting of the location or timing of land-use change or development activities. The real challenge is to move towards the incorporation of positive elements. The legislative duty on some sectors to take account of nature conservation provides some potential, as does the increasing interest by industry, often for commercial reasons. The requirement is to convert sometimes complex ecological information to simple but sound prescriptions, to permit links with other sectoral policies.

Some of the biggest opportunities lie in agricultural policy, both because of its role as the dominant land-use and because policies are in a state of change, with public support for environmentally friendly measures. There is both the potential to maintain the high wildlife value in remaining extensively farmed areas and reverse some of the losses of recent intensification. It has been concluded that "the single most important cause of species decline is habitat change, and it is the increasing intensity, scale and dynamism of human activities which are chiefly responsible for the degradation of natural and semi-natural habitats in Europe". In Britain, more than 50% of farmland bird species contracted in range in the twenty years between 1970 and 1990, while hardly any expanded.

In recent years, some of these effects have become recognised, and attempts made to reverse them. The Game Conservancy's work on grey partridges, their insect prey and plants, as well as the potential for these and other species of unsprayed "headlands" around cropped fields have become well known. The benefits of traditional farming methods to corncrakes and ecologically related species have been incorporated in co-operative schemes between crofters and farmers and conservation bodies including Royal Society for the Protection of Birds, the Department of the Environment for Northern Ireland and Scottish Natural Heritage. Other schemes in the UK include Environmentally Sensitive Areas, the Countryside Stewardship Scheme run by the Countryside Commission in England and Tir Cymen (which translates as a well composed landscape) of the Countryside Council for Wales.

However, many conservationists have expressed regret that the major schemes to reduce agricultural over-production in the EC, such as "set-aside" have few environmental elements, and may even be environmentally damaging in some circumstances. For example, the Third European Forum on Nature Conservation and Pastoralism in July 1992 concluded that, in the four years that it had been meeting, it could report no reversal in the trend of decline of extensive agro-pastoral systems and predicted a worsening situation. It considered that many rare and endangered species of plants and animals (and human communities) associated with these systems, and protected by European law, are being lost through the application of some elements of the Common Agricultural Policy (CAP) and other EC-wide policy measures. EC policies are not integrated and are sometimes contradictory.

There is a need for clear, scientifically and practicably based guidance from conservation bodies to land-use policy makers, in order to fulfil the environmental potential presented by changes in EC agricultural policies. This need was expressed by the then UK Minister of Agriculture, Mr John Selwyn Gummer, at a seminar on "A future for Europe's farmed countryside" in Cambridge in September 1992, organised by RSPB, the Department of the Environment and the Ministry of Agriculture, Fisheries & Food.

One of the most important ways of conserving biological diversity is by maintaining and restoring characteristic regional features. There is a need to zone the country to some extent, because measures appropriate for nature conservation and farming in one region could be totally inappropriate for both in another. Eight broad land-type zones have been identified in Great Britain, to assist the linking of national and international land-use policies and regional practices, particularly agricultural, to the wildlife interest that these affect. These zones are based on environmentally imposed potential rather than actual land-use or vegetation cover. The zones should therefore have some stability. The distribution of these zones has been compared with the distributions of bird assemblages to illustrate their relevance to nature conservation. As a pointer to future work needs, that publication links examples of main actual and potential nature conservation interest to farming enterprises and the agricultural policies which underlie these.

4. ACHIEVING BIODIVERSITY OBJECTIVES WITHIN THE COUNTRY CONSERVATION AGENCIES

4.1   Action Plan objectives

The publication of *Biodiversity: the UK Action Plan* set objectives and targets to guide the work of the Government and its agencies over the following 20 years. A substantial part of the implementation of this plan will fall to the statutory nature conservation agencies, the Countryside Council for Wales (CCW), English Nature (EN), Scottish Natural Heritage (SNH) and Department of the Environment for Northern Ireland, with some of the co-ordination work undertaken by the staff of the Joint Nature Conservation Committee (JNCC).

The Plan lists 59 items under a heading "progress towards objectives". Preliminary assessment suggests that one or more of the country agencies will have a major role in achieving at least 25 of these. Other Government agencies may be expected to have a lead role or make a significant contribution in 39. Even for these, the conservation agencies can expect to be involved, either by providing advice (assisted where necessary by appropriate research) or by seeking to influence or encourage others. Twenty six items, at least, will involve the JNCC. In only five do the country agencies appear to have little or no role. These divisions are not mutually exclusive and the achievement of some "progress towards objectives" items may require action by the different agencies in a number of roles.

Few of the "progress towards objectives" items give any indication of the timescale within which they are to be achieved, though work on this is in hand through the Biodiversity Action Plan Steering Committee and its sub-committees. Topics considered by these sub-committees are preparation of detailed plan targets, determination of data requirements, and raising the awareness and involvement of the public. Each committee has representatives from Government, each of the country agencies, voluntary bodies, local authorities and academia, and provides an opportunity to debate and influence the continuing development of the Plan. The publication of *Biodiversity Challenge, an agenda for conservation in the UK* by a consortium of voluntary bodies is a significant contribution in this respect (see Chapter 6). At this stage, the country agencies are formally considering their locus within each objective and the means by which they may implement appropriate action. The process of preparing annual and medium-term work programmes and strategic plans is on-going; these plans will have to remain flexible to take account of new targets and to encompass the long term forward look of the Action Plan. The objectives, nevertheless, encompass a broad range of the traditional, routine work of the country agencies, such as site-safeguard, along with new initiatives and programmes. Other objectives will require a re-deployment and prioritisation of effort if they are to be achieved.

4.2   Protected areas

Significantly, the first three "progress towards objectives" of the plan relate to protected areas and site safeguard, including Sites of Special Scientific Interest (SSSI), notified under the 1981 Wildlife & Countryside Act (as amended), Special Protection Areas (SPA) classified under European Communities Directive 79/409 on the Conservation of Wild Birds and Special Areas of Conservation yet to be classified under EC Directive 92/43 on the Conservation of Natural Habitats and of Wild Fauna and Flora.

With more than 6000 SSSIs (in GB) or ASSIs (Areas of Special Scientific Interest in Northern Ireland) in the UK (Box 4.1), the production of summary management

---

Box 4.1   Number and area (in 1000s hectares) of protected areas within the UK at 30 November 1994

Country	SSSI or ASSI		Ramsar		SPA		NNR		% land area within
	No.	Area	No.	Area	No.	Area	No.	Area	SSSI/ASSI
England	3812	875	48	221	50	261	157	61	6.7
Scotland	1377	856	24	47	32	61	70	114	11.1
Wales	892	206	7	18	8	19	53	16	9.9
N Ireland	65	62	1	39	2	0	45	5	4.4
TOTAL	6147	1999	80	325	92	341	325	196	8.2

SSSI or ASSI = Site (or in N Ireland, Area) of Special Scientific Interest; the area of SSSI/ASSI includes those of the other three designations.
Ramsar = Sites listed under the "Ramsar" Convention on Wetlands of International Importance.
SPA = Special Protection Area classified under the European Community Directive 79/409 on the Conservation of Wild Birds.
NNR = National Nature Reserve.

plans for each site of biological interest ("progress towards objectives" 1), even by 2004, is a major task. Whilst many of these SSSIs are notified for their earth science interest alone, in Scotland sites of biological or joint interest account for 76% of the total number. No new SSSI is notified by SNH without a summary management plan first being produced, and SNH aims to achieve plan production for existing sites within ten years. Similarly, EN aims to complete statements of objectives for all SSSIs initially, with management statements thereafter. Implementation of plans depends on the availability of resources and the willingness of owners and occupiers to undertake positive management. There are more than 8,000 owners and occupiers on the 1,377 SSSIs in Scotland, and SNH has a rolling programme of contacting at least 20% of these per annum in order to initiate dialogue over management. Even so, only 517 management agreements have been concluded (covering almost 14% of SSSI area), along with 58 agreements or leases covering National Nature Reserves. To expedite the positive management of protected areas, a number of schemes have been initiated by each of the agencies to streamline the process of achieving agreement and to seek maximum return for resources. These include EN's Reserve Enhancement scheme, CCW's Berwyn SSSI and Tir Cymen scheme and SNH's Peatland Management scheme in Caithness and Sutherland and Merse Management scheme on the Solway Firth.

The formal designation of sites under international agreements or directives, such as SPAs and Ramsar sites, is done by the appropriate Secretary of State. However, the country agencies are responsible for the original SSSI notification, for consultation with owners, occupiers and Local Planning Authorities and for preparing a detailed brief for the site. The current SPAs and Ramsar sites are part of an ongoing selection and designation process. Implementation of the Habitats Directive within the agencies has so far concentrated on the selection of potential sites. A list of these sites was published in 1995 for later submission to the European Commission. In all these cases the selection of the sites has involved close inter-agency working, co-ordinated by JNCC staff. In order to meet the European timetable, work relating to the notification and designation of SACs is likely to take high priority for the country agencies over the next 10 years. For example, implementation of this work within SNH is being achieved by the creation of a Natura 2000 project team involving the recruitment of 19 new staff. Within this process, gaps in the existing coverage of the SSSI network, such as rivers and marine sites ("progress towards objectives" 2), are likely to be filled to comply with the requirements of the Directive.

Significant research, survey and evaluation effort is usually required to inform the selection and management of SSSIs. Whilst protected areas have proved to be an effective mechanism for the maintenance of the features for which they were selected, their significance for the overall maintenance of biodiversity, especially for the less well-known but numerically large groups of invertebrates and lower plants, has not been tested. The representation of some groups has had to rely in part on their chance occurrence on sites selected on other grounds. "Hotspots" for one taxon do not necessarily identify important areas for other taxa. It is therefore important that the role of the protected area network in conserving overall biodiversity should be assessed critically.

The selection and representation of protected areas may need to be considered in a biogeographic framework. Such a framework can also aid the setting of targets for particular species or habitats, contribute to the feeling of "a sense of place" and enable comparative analyses within defined zones. Accordingly, EN have identified and described 76 natural areas and 23 maritime areas based on an assessment of the biological and physical characters of the landscape. This concept has been developed rather differently in Scotland by the commission of an analysis of biogeographic zones undertaken by the Environmental Information Centre at Monks Wood, and based on datasets of selected groups of organisms ("progress towards objectives" 8, 45).

4.3   Wider countryside

Whereas objectives for protected areas require a direct involvement of the country agencies, their role in other objectives may be to advise or influence others. This applies especially to land-use, such as agriculture, forestry and fisheries, in the "wider countryside" beyond protected areas. The country agencies' role is also to help other incentives operating in the wider countryside to maintain biodiversity. This may involve advising on the selection and management of Environmentally Sensitive Areas (ESAs) or responding to consultations over applications to the Forestry Authority's Woodland Grant Scheme (WGS).

The agencies also have a major advisory role in ensuring that biodiversity is considered fully in development control. For example, this may involve contributing advice and information to Local Planning Authorities on the development of structure and local plans, and responding to consultations over planning applications. The development of indicative forest strategies in Scotland has enabled SNH, in collaboration with JNCC, to influence the future siting and design of forest plantations to avoid areas of high conservation or landscape interest (see Chapter 3).

A major means of influencing and encouraging the actions of others is by entering into partnerships or awarding grant-aid. During 1992/3 SNH contributed £940,000 to the Central Scotland Woodland Countryside Trust for the creation of multi-purpose woodlands, both to improve a degraded environment and to restore biodiversity across parts of central Scotland ("progress towards objectives" 31). In conjunction with the Forestry Authority, Highlands and Islands Enterprise and

Highland Regional Council, SNH are able to promote the spread of native woodland cover, through the Highland Birchwoods scheme, more effectively than any partner could do alone ("progress towards objectives" 29). A similar project, Coed Cymri, operates in Wales with the support of CCW. The Farming & Wildlife Advisory Groups rely on a major element of grant support from the country conservation agencies, yet they are a cost effective means of delivering conservation advice to farmers, thus complementing the work of ADAS (formerly the Agricultural Development & Advisory Service) and the Scottish Agricultural College ("progress towards objectives" 22).

Emphasis on the marine, inter-tidal and coastal environment, hitherto a largely neglected area, is a notable feature of objectives in the Plan. EN's estuaries programme and SNH's "Focus on Firths" initiative both seek to produce management plans for estuaries based on a co-operative approach with other users of the areas ("progress towards objectives" 12). Whilst many of these sites attract a range of designations, from SSSIs, Ramsar sites, and National Scenic Areas to Biosphere reserves, the approach is to secure a consensus on future management that will sustain both the natural heritage interest and human use of it, whether for fisheries, wildfowling or tourism. Such initiatives inevitably contribute to the attainment of a number of objectives. The Focus on Firths initiative encourages involvement of people in the conservation of "their" estuary, produces materials that can be used for environmental education, and encourages the interpretation of sites to visitors and locals alike ("progress towards objectives" 43, 44 & 45). Research projects range from landscape assessments to work on individual species, such as bottle-nosed dolphins in the Moray Firth, which may contribute to further Action Plan objectives (e.g. "progress towards objectives" 33, 41 & 55).

Support is continuing for marine nature reserves ("progress towards objectives" 15), such as the voluntary reserve at St. Abb's Head or the statutory one at Skomer. In future, though, the mechanisms for delivery of marine conservation may rely upon the new Regulations enacted to implement the requirements of the Habitats Directive ("progress towards objectives" 11). Whilst fishery research is undertaken by the appropriate Government Departments and their laboratories, it may fall to the country agencies to be involved in determining the effects of particular fishing practices on the natural heritage ("progress towards objectives" 38). The recent expansion of the tractor- and boat-based cockle fishery, for example, prompted collaborative research between the country agencies into the effects of this fishery on non-target organisms and the potential knock-on effects on wintering bird populations.

4.4   Species

For species conservation, the most far reaching "progress towards objectives" (33) in the UK Plan relates to the production of action plans for threatened species in a defined priority order. With the exception of those plans produced for birds, pioneered by Royal Society for the Protection of Birds (RSPB) in collaboration with JNCC and the country agencies, the production of species action plans has hitherto been sporadic and *ad hoc*.

Box 4.2   A preliminary assessment of species occurring in Scotland and considered to be threatened globally or to be   endemic   and threatened; endemic species in bold type, species in parentheses considered to be extinct in Britain

---

Fungi: *Tulostoma niveum*

Lichens: *Collema dichotomum*, Schistmatoma graphidiodes*

Bryophytes: ***Bryoerythrophyllum caledonicum; (Bryum lawersianum);*** *Gymnostonum insigne; Lejeuna mandonii;* ***Pictus scoticus; Pohlia scotica; Sphagnum skyense; (Tortella limosella)***

Vascular plants: *Artemisia norvegica;* ***Athyrium flexile; Calamagrostis scotica; Cerastium nigrescens; Cochlearia micacea, Epipactis youngiana*,*** *Euphrasia (5 spp.);* ***(Sagina boydii); Senecio cambrensis;*** *Trichomanes speciosum*.*

Invertebrates: *Formica aquilona; Formica lugubris; Hirudo medicinalis; Margaritifera margaritifera; Vertigo angustior.*

Herpetofauna: Marine turtles Cheloniidae & Dermochelyidae (4 species)*.

Birds: Red kite *Milvus milvus;* sea eagle *Haliaeetus albicilla;* corncrake *Crex crex*,* **Scottish crossbill *Loxia scotica*.***

Mammals: Whales & dolphins Cetacea* (12 regular spp., 13 vagrants).

* — species given special protection under the Wildlife & Countryside Act by their inclusion on schedules 1, 5 or 8.

In Scotland alone there are over 180 species that fall into the top three priority classes of the UK Action Plan (namely globally threatened, threatened endemics, and species on schedules of the Wildlife & Countryside Act and on the Annexes of international agreements) but only 47 in the two uppermost categories of these (Box 4.2). These totals increase substantially if the additional species in Red Data Books and Lists are included. For a number of species, survey and/or monitoring will be required to establish their current status, and autecological research will be essential to elucidate what action is required, if any, to maintain or restore populations of the species concerned. SNH has recently initiated a 3-year research programme which will result in the production of action plans for all threatened vascular plant species in Scotland, the work involving all the elements identified above. The production of bird action plans is being done jointly by the RSPB and agencies and work is also in progress on the 33 species of protected lower plants that occur in Scotland. It is hoped to extend this programme to the endemic and globally threatened lower plants and threatened invertebrates over the coming years.

The Action Plan priorities also require the agencies to address the needs of species that might not previously have been considered priorities. This may include a number which are not currently given legal protection (Box 4.2). World Red Data Lists, produced by the World Conservation Monitoring Centre (WCMC) or International Union for the Conservation of Nature (IUCN), from which globally threatened species are identified, contain a high proportion of endemic species. The taxonomy of many of these species in the UK is still subject to debate and these issues may need to be resolved before we can progress action. Further, it is likely that these WCMC lists will continue to change as more information on the world status of species becomes available. In terms of conserving genetic biodiversity, however, is it of major significance if the organism we seek to conserve is considered by some taxonomists to be an endemic species, for example Newman's lady fern *Athyrium flexile*, or to be an endemic variety, *Athyrium distentifolium* var. *flexile*, by others? On the other hand, if legal protection is seen as a mechanism to contribute to the conservation of the organism, then it is vital that there is no confusion over its taxonomic status and identification.

Implementation of some of these plans in SNH has already begun for some species, notably the three globally threatened birds. The current re-introduction programme for the sea eagle is now in its 19th year and is likely to continue for some years yet, whilst the more recent programme for red kites, initiated by RSPB and JNCC, will move into further phases. Likewise, SNH is an active partner with RSPB in the corncrake initiative involving grant payments to farmers to cut fields in a "corncrake-friendly" manner and to delay cutting dates. Whilst these species are relatively high profile, other work has involved the recovery of the New Forest burnet moth *Zygaena viciae* subsp. *argyllensis* and research into twaite shad *Alosa alosa* and allis shad *A. fallax*. The annual spend in SNH on programmes relating to species conservation exceeded £250,000 in 1993/94 and is planned to increase with the development of a co-ordinated species action programme. English Nature's Species Recovery Programme ("progress towards objectives" 34), with an annual

---

**Box 4.3   Species included in English Nature's Species Recovery
Programme with an assessment of current progress**

Progress: *Species*

Completed: Rough marsh-mallow *Althaea hirsuta;* starfruit *Damasomium
alisma*; Essex emerald moth *Thetidia smaragradia;* large copper
butterfly *Lycaena dispar.*

Final stages: Strapwort *Corrigiola littoralis*; Plymouth pear *Pyrus cordata*;
ribbon-leaved water plantain *Alisma gramineum*; fen raft spider
Dolomedes plantarius.

Ongoing: Brecklands lichens (3 spp.); fen violet *Viola persicifolia*; stinking
hawk's beard *Crepis foetida*; lady's slipper orchid *Cypripedium
calceolus*; wart biter cricket Decticus verrucivorous; field cricket
Gryllus compestris; New Forest cicada *Cicadetta montana*; reddish
buff moth *Acosmetia caliginosa;* large *blue butterfly Maculinea
arion,* spangled water beetle *Graphoderus zonatus*; lagoon
sandworm *Armandia cirrhosa*; natterjack toad *Bufo calamita*;
dormouse *Muscardinus* avellanarius; red squirrel *Sciurus vulgaris.*

New projects: Shore dock *Rumex rupestris*; perennial knawel *Scleranthus perennis*
ssp. *protratus*; ground pine *Ajuga chamaepitys;* fen orchid *Liparis
loesellii,* ladybird spider *Eresus cinnaberinus*; sand lizard *Lacerta
agilis*; smooth snake *Coronella austriaca*; bittern *Botaurus stellarus*;
greater horseshoe bat *Rhinolophus ferrumequinum*; pine marten
Martes martes.

---

budget of £390,000, deals with a rolling programme of species (Box 4.3). Action
has been completed for 4 species, and is in progress on 18 others with new projects
initiated for a further 10 species. CCW are to initiate work on the recovery of the
fen orchid *Liparis loeselii*. Increasingly future research work needs to focus on the
management of the small, isolated populations that are typical of many of our
threatened species, especially where translocations are involved or material is being
taken into, or returned from, *ex situ* conservation ("progress towards objectives" 36,
37).

The implementation of Action Plans, through programmes such as these, are not
only an effective means of maintaining or restoring elements of our biota but can
also help raise awareness of the meaning and importance of biodiversity. It is vital
that these programmes are properly planned and co-ordinated and that they have
targets and indicators by which to evaluate success or, alternatively, to determine
when continued effort can no longer be justified.

4.5   Public awareness

One of the functions of the statutory conservation agencies is to aid people's "understanding and enjoyment" of the natural heritage. This ties in with one of the key areas of the Action Plan, and encompasses a broad spectrum of the work of the agencies. SNH has provided an input to the Scottish Working Party on Environmental Education and has started a formal project concerned with the delivery of environmental education. "Grounds for Learning" is a partnership project derived from this initiative aimed at enhancing school grounds to further their potential for education including, but not exclusively, raising awareness of the natural environment ("progress towards objectives" 47). Other projects may range from creating and interpreting local nature reserves, through the publication of leaflets and educational material to wider environmental improvement schemes but in which nature conservation plays a prominent role. Nineteen such projects have been undertaken as part of SNH's Countryside Around Towns programme, with most of these in Scotland's central belt ("progress towards objectives" 17, 45).

5. BIODIVERSITY AND THE ROLE OF LOCAL AUTHORITIES

5.1 Introduction

Local authorities have a central role and one of the most important responsibilities for biodiversity – ensuring that development is sensitive to the environment. However local authority action on biodiversity is not confined to statutory forward planning and development control.

In addition to statutory planning duties, direct action by local authorities includes the management for nature conservation of their own land, including Country Parks, school grounds, Local Nature Reserves and other areas such as coastal land. Many local authorities own, or have a long lease, on land designated as SSSI or NNR. Local authorities are also assisting others to manage land for nature conservation through the provision of grant-aid and advice, and the establishment of major habitat management projects covering wide geographical areas, such as the restoration of heathlands and coppice woods in southern England.

Local authorities often act as the link or co-ordinator for nature conservation projects. Many have set up nature conservation fora involving a wide range of statutory and voluntary bodies. Most have prepared nature conservation strategies to direct their own work and to help influence others. Sometimes these are compiled in partnership with other bodies such as country conservation agencies and the Wildlife Trusts.

There are many examples where local authorities assist and empower other bodies to achieve biodiversity objectives. These include: provision of grant-aid to support Wildlife Trusts, provision of advice to the Forestry Authority on grant and felling licence applications, provision of advice to the National Rivers Authority on Catchment Management Plans, directing landowners into national habitat management grant schemes, and the employment of officers for Areas of Outstanding Natural Beauty.

Local authorities often hold the main biological database for their area, providing a comprehensive data service either from a records centre or an individual department, and many use geographical information systems. Data and their interpretation are fundamental in achieving biodiversity objectives.

The influence that local authorities can exert ranges from affecting central government thinking on national policy, legislation and advice, to meeting local needs and engaging the local community in action for biodiversity. Such action may include the establishment of community nature areas, grant support for community projects, caring for local areas, and the establishment of communication networks for voluntary bodies.

5.2   A fundamental responsibility – sustainable development

The most fundamental responsibility of local authorities for biodiversity is the planning and control of development. The search for measures and procedures to ensure development is sustainable is a major challenge, and one which is inextricably linked with biodiversity. The rest of this chapter focuses on the responsibility of local authorities for conserving habitats and species through development plans and development control (the processing of planning applications).

The chapter reviews three elements considered essential for this process:

- Evaluation of the nature conservation resource (estimation, classification, evaluation);

- Classification of the relative importance of sites/areas to aid forward planning and development control decisions;

- Development plan policies to ensure appropriate levels of protection of the biological resource.

The current emphasis on sustainable development has set new standards, requiring a particularly disciplined approach to evaluation and policy preparation. Systems for evaluating the nature conservation resource and for guiding decisions need to be robust and to stand up to the closest scrutiny. It should also be possible to use them to monitor whether sustainable development objectives are being met. Standards involve, for example, undertaking appropriately timed surveys in a replicated manner, in order to control for normal variation in wildlife populations and to understand biases of surveys. Survey standards are then used to evaluate the data against published sources, 1% biogeographic population levels, indices of abundance or rarity, etc. The approach outlined below is based on the most recent thinking on sustainable development.

5.3   Evaluating the nature conservation resource

Some local plans include two main policies for nature conservation; one which gives general regard to the intention to conserve the resource as a whole, while the second policy gives added weight to protecting statutory designated areas. However, it is widely acknowledged that such a distinction is not refined enough to help achieve sustainable development (indeed it is woefully inadequate). The statutory sites are only those of national or international importance and, in the case of SSSIs, represent only "examples" of national importance; they do not represent all that is of critical importance for nature conservation.

Attention is often given to statutory sites at the expense of the much larger area of critical nature conservation resource. Outside the statutory sites, there are many sites of national or regional importance for nature conservation and extensive areas of semi-natural habitat that, once lost, cannot be recreated. It is, therefore, common practice for Local Authorities to identify and designate such additional important sites in their development plans. Most county councils and unitary authorities have their own non-statutory site designation system, sometimes developed in partnership with the local Wildlife Trust, the country conservation agency or both. Some district councils have their own system but usually subscribe to the county system.

Local authority systems for defining sites of importance vary considerably, and local authorities use a variety of titles for the sites identified. One title gaining particular currency is Sites of Importance for Nature Conservation (SINCs). This term will be used throughout the rest of this paper for convenience.

5.4   Site designation – classifying nature conservation importance

The criteria and measures used by local authorities to evaluate the nature

---

Box 5.1   Criteria used for evaluating nature conservation importance

Evaluation of SSSIs

Size
Diversity
Rarity
Naturalness
Fragility
Typicalness
History
Position in ecological/geographical unit
Potential value
Intrinsic appeal

Examples of additional criteria used by local authorities

Important populations of species (may also be used to evaluate SSSIs)
Access (physical and visual)
Educational value
Situated in an area of deficiency

---

conservation interest of sites vary. Most local authorities use an adaptation of the criteria used for identification of SSSIs (Box 5.1).

A more difficult procedure is to classify sites in terms of their relative importance. Scoring systems or the subjective allocation of "high", "medium" and "low" values to the site attributes listed in Box 5.1 are often used to help grade sites. Resulting site classifications are sometimes based on grades of importance, such as Grades 1, 2 and 3, or have a geographical basis, such as sites of County, District and Local Importance. However such hierarchical site designation systems present problems. It is difficult to define thresholds between categories clearly, or to differentiate the relative protection to be applied to each category; and yet further sub-division runs the risk of totally devaluing the lower categories.

Because of these problems, the more favoured approach is the definition of a single category of site which justifies particularly strong protection. The rest of the nature conservation resource remains undesignated but is usually covered by an appropriate nature conservation policy in the development plan.

The difficulties remaining here are:

• how should the threshold for designation be determined?

• are there any objective measures for determining the threshold?

• do thresholds have to vary depending on the quantity and quality of the nature conservation resource in different local authority areas?

After 15 years of developing site designation systems, local authorities are probably now at a watershed in terms of how to overcome the above problems in defining sites of particular importance. A new approach incorporating sustainable development is being adopted by Hampshire County Council during its review of the County Structure Plan and is explained below. It is based on the sustainable development concept of Critical Natural Capital.

5.5 Critical natural capital – a new basis for site designation

Critical natural capital consists of those assets (habitats or species) that are effectively irreplaceable. It is a term now in common usage at local authority level. A good example of critical natural capital is ancient semi-natural woodland. Critical natural capital cannot be recreated and, if spent, is lost for ever. It therefore justifies the strongest conservation measures.

English Nature has published a policy statement on sustainable development which commits it to oppose development and land-use which adversely and irreversibly affect critical natural capital. It is implicit that there should be no policy distinction in development plans between the protection given to statutory designated sites and those sites which constitute the remainder of the critical natural capital. All are above the threshold of critical importance (irreplaceable), although it can be accepted that there is a gradation of importance within critical natural capital.

Critical natural capital is a sound basis for local authority site designation, and can be defined as "habitat which is irreplaceable, biologically or socially, within a reasonable timescale and in practice." However, what exactly is irreplaceable? Some consider that critical natural capital should be based on minimum areas of viable habitat needed to support viable populations, rather than including all habitat that is irreplaceable. However, this might be considered a seriously harmful approach. Much more preferable is an approach to defining critical natural capital that is pragmatic and precautionary. With a small degree of pragmatism, it is easy to define what is irreplaceable and conclude that all the irreplaceable resource should be defined as critical natural capital rather than a proportion of it.

For example, Hampshire County Council has established a detailed set of criteria against which to identify the irreplaceable critical resource beyond the statutory sites (ie including SINCs). Examples of habitats meeting the criteria include all ancient semi-natural woodland, unimproved chalk grassland and sites supporting rare species.

When evaluating the nature conservation importance of sites, it is also important to consider social factors. For example, sites may be important as an educational resource, or be located in an area otherwise deficient in wildlife sites for public enjoyment. It is just as important to identify sites that are critically important for social reasons as those which are important for their ecological characteristics per se. Defining sites of critical social importance tends to involve more subjectivity. Pragmatism again must be involved in attaching the label of "critical" to sites in areas severely deficient in sites of natural interest available to the public, or where there is a high degree of community investment into a site – such as an urban wildlife area managed by the community. These are obviously situations that are practically very difficult to recreate.

Box 5.2 In summary the biological resource can be divided as follows:

Statutory sites (eg SSSIs) SINCs

Rest of the nature

|-------------------------------------|

conservation resource

Critical Natural Capital
(with strongest protection measures)

5.6   Maintaining biodiversity beyond the designated sites

Beyond the critical resource, there is a large stock of habitat which is important for nature conservation and which contributes to the fabric of environmental quality. For example, beyond Hampshire County Council's definition of critical natural capital lies most of the County's secondary woodland, ponds, hedgerows and semi-improved grassland. It is essential that appropriate protection for this stock of habitat is provided in development plans.

A useful concept for considering the protection of these sites is the sustainable development concept of "constant natural assets". This means that the loss of, or damage to, a particular site or feature of interest may be permissible in certain circumstances, but the aim should be to maintain a constant level of net natural assets. This means that loss or damage of habitats should be compensated for by provision of new habitat or enhancement of existing habitat. This concept does not carry with it a presumption that an area of nature conservation interest which does not reach the standard for SINC or statutory designation can be damaged or destroyed in favour of replacement. Indeed, damage or loss should be resisted and accepted only in overriding circumstances.

Within this nature conservation resource, there is a gradation of nature conservation value and the ability of a site to accept damage or be replaced. All development proposals affecting these sites should be considered on their merits.

Department of the Environment Circular Advice 16/91 on Planning Obligations provides a means by which the overall quality and quantity of natural assets can be secured for future generations. The Circular states that it is reasonable for a local planning authority to seek from a developer measures which offset the loss of, or impact on, an amenity or resource present on site prior to development, for example in the interests of nature conservation. This could include agreements to establish habitats within or adjacent to the development, secured through legal agreements and conditions on planning permission.

5.7   Enhancing biodiversity

Whether loss or damage of habitat is involved or not, a sound principle for development is to enhance the nature conservation resource wherever possible. This helps to maintain the net level of natural assets, but should also be used as an approach which strives for a net increase in natural assets. Examples of opportunities for development to enhance biodiversity include the restoration and after-use of mineral workings and the landscaping and management of open space developments such as golf courses.

Box 5.3   A sustainable approach to biodiversity

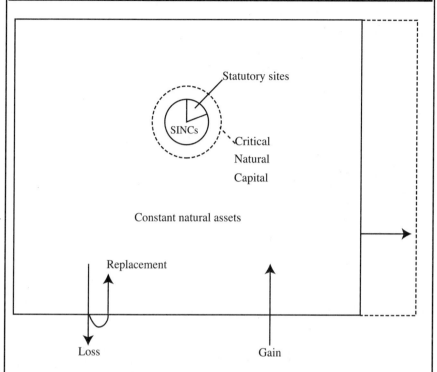

Development plan policies for biodiversity

Policy 1   Maintain all CRITICAL NATURAL CAPITAL

Development will not be permitted which will have an adverse effect on SSSIs and SINCs.

Policy 2   Maintain a net level of NATURAL ASSETS

Development will not normally be permitted which will adversely affect other sites of nature conservation interest. Where development is permitted which affects nature conservation interest, provision shall be made for replacement or substitution of habitats or features where appropriate.

Policy 3   ENHANCE the biological resource where possible

When granting permission, the opportunity shall be taken to create or improve habitats and features of nature conservation interest, where appropriate.

5.8 Review of the approach and development plan policies

Box 5.3 summarises the approach outlined above for maintaining biodiversity through the forward planning and development control process, with relevant development plan policies.

Thus, Critical Natural Capital comprises all the statutory designated sites and the rest of the irreplaceable nature conservation resource. The critical natural capital beyond the statutory sites should be defined and designated by local authorities in their development plans – and these plans should presume against development affecting critical natural capital.

The rest of the nature conservation resource should at least be maintained at a net level (constant natural assets), and the aim should be to increase this level through sensitively planned development. Inevitably, there may be losses without direct compensation, but there should also be gains that are independent of losses.

Habitat management outside the planning process can help maintain and increase the level of critical and constant natural capital.

6. BIODIVERSITY AND THE VOLUNTARY SECTOR

6.1   Introduction

In December 1993 (prior to the Government publishing its Biodiversity Plan), a consortium of voluntary conservation bodies produced a document called *Biodiversity Challenge*. Its aim was to assist the Government and to show that, despite the many varied organisations involved, a unanimous purpose existed among the voluntary nature conservation bodies. The approach was that of demonstrating the need to establish appropriate targets, together with some of the steps to achieve them. The document aimed to represent the concerns of a combined membership of the voluntary bodies of over 2 million people. The challenge of the document's title was to halt the decline in biodiversity in the UK and to recoup at least some of our present losses. In 1995, the consortium published a second edition of *Biodiversity Challenge* which is intended to help take forward the Government's *Biodiversity: the UK Action Plan* (published in 1994) and address many of the challenges set by the plan, drawing on the knowledge of dozens of experts across the conservation spectrum.

6.2   The *Biodiversity Challenge* approach

The overall goal of *Biodiversity Challenge* is to conserve and enhance biological diversity within the UK, and to contribute to the conservation of global biodiversity through all available mechanisms.

The approach developed by the six voluntary conservation bodies (Butterfly Conservation, Friends of the Earth, Plantlife, the Royal Society for the Protection of Birds, The Wildlife Trusts, and the World Wide Fund for Nature) involves a number of key elements which include:

Audit to assess what we have in the UK in terms of biodiversity involving species and habitats;

Goal, objectives and measurable species and habitat targets;

Priorities which acknowledge that resources are limited and time to effect action plans is short;

Implementation, involving species and habitat action plans and generic actions;

Monitoring and review arrangements which represent the essential feedback loop necessary to assess the progress of the action plans.

Box 6.1   The objectives of *Biodiversity Challenge*

- To maintain and enhance the populations and natural ranges of species and the quality and extent of wildlife habitats and ecosystems.

- To conserve internationally important species, habitats and ecosystems and enhance their conservation status where possible.

- To conserve threatened species, habitats and ecosystems and enhance their conservation status where possible.

- To conserve species, habitats and natural managed ecosystems that are characteristic of local areas and enhance their conservation status where possible.

- To restore valued ecosystems where they have been degraded and to prevent further degradation of all ecosystems by maintaining ecological processes.

- To maintain genetic variation within species and hence habitats and ecosystems.

- To contribute to the conservation of biodiversity on a European and global scale.

- To ensure that UK policies and practices which affect the environment beyond the limits of national jurisdiction do not damage biodiversity but instead contribute towards conserving and enhancing it.

6.3   Targets for species and habitats

Conservation targets refine the overall objectives in terms of biological results which can be measured or assessed. Targets help to clarify the aims, and are also necessary to identify the successes and failures. National targets for species and habitats are suggested in the *Biodiversity Challenge* document, abstracts of which are presented in this chapter.

To set conservation targets the following guidelines have been adopted.

Species targets should:

a) be realistic but ambitious;

b) refer to a period of about the next 10 years;

c) be quantitative in terms of population numbers and/or range.

Examples of targets might be to maintain numbers and/or ranges at stated current levels, to increase numbers to new stated levels within the natural range of the species or to restore numbers and ranges to stated previous levels as defined by monitoring.

Likewise, habitats targets should:

a) be realistic but ambitious;

b) refer to a period of about the next 10 years;

c) be quantitative in terms of habitat extent;

d) be quantitative in terms of habitat quality where this can be defined in terms of, for example, the state of the associated flora and fauna or physico-chemical habitat aspects.

Examples of targets might be to maintain habitat extent at existing stated levels, restore the area of the habitat to a formerly attained stated level, increase the area of the habitat by a certain amount which meets a stated level of habitat quality, for example double the area with pollution levels lower than a set amount. Habitat conservation targets should incorporate species targets and resolve any conflicts of interest. Most importantly, these targets should encompass the requirements of all species within the habitat, balancing the rare and common species across all taxa.

6.4   Priorities

The focus is to direct limited conservation resources towards those species which need conservation action the most. Most recently, identification of species of high priority for conservation action has been through the production of Red Data books. On a global scale these are produced by the IUCN and deal with those species most endangered by extinction – the globally threatened species. Several Red Data books have been produced covering Britain or the UK or Britain and Ireland, and others are in preparation, dealing with rare, localised and declining species and endemic species within the UK and/or species of international importance. *Biodiversity Challenge* identifies that Red Data book species are not more important than other species; they are simply species which need more or urgent conservation action. Theoretically species enter and leave Red Data book status as their fortunes change, with the aim being to improve the status of rare and threatened ones so that eventually they are no longer included.

6.5   Setting conservation targets

Targets should be set for species which qualify under any of the following categories (placed in approximate order of priority):

- Species endemic to the British Isles or the UK;

- Species threatened with global extinction;

- Species for which the UK holds an internationally important proportion of the European population;

- Species which are rapidly declining in numbers or range. Declines of more than 50% since 1960 in numbers or range, e.g. size of breeding population or number of occupied 10 km squares, could be used as yard-sticks. The interpretation of this guideline might differ across taxa;

- Species which are rare or localised, e.g. plants or insects restricted to fewer than 15 10 km squares, birds whose breeding populations number fewer than 300 pairs and birds with over half their population found in fewer than 10 sites;

- Species which have become extinct in the UK since 1900.

Targets should be set for habitats which qualify under any of the following categories (not in priority order):

- Habitats on which priority species depend;

- Habitats for which the UK holds an important proportion of the total world or European resource;

- Habitats rapidly declining in area;

- Habitats declining in quality;

- Habitats which are rare, i.e. of limited area;

- Habitats which are listed on Annex I of the EU Habitats and Species Directive.

Biodiversity Challenge suggests that a UK habitat Red Data book is needed since the approach to habitat priorities in the UK is much less well developed than for species priorities. It is intended that the targets in *Biodiversity Challenge* should be seen as performance indicators for the UK, and that the conservation organisations will be reminding the Government of these conservation targets in the future.

6.6   Implementing a Plan for Action

Box 6.2   Underlying principles which *Biodiversity Challenge* identified

---

a)   Biological resources must be used sustainably;

b)   Non-renewable resources must be used wisely;

c)   Conservation policy and practice must stem from a sound knowledge base;

d)   Biodiversity conservation must be an integral part of all Government programmes, policy and action at national and local levels;

e)   The precautionary principle must guide all decisions which could cause environmental damage;

f)   Environmental appraisal and economic appraisal must be widely carried out at both a strategic and project level;

g)   Regulation which controls matters such as site protection and pollution must be used to prevent biodiversity losses below critical levels;

h)   Economic measures may be preferred to regulations to achieve higher environmental standards within sustainable limits;

i)   Subsidies which lead to a loss of biodiversity must be removed,

j)   Biodiversity conservation requires the care and involvement of individuals and communities as well as government process;

k)   The lessons of the past must be learned. There are enough examples of ecological damage caused by human actions to avoid a repetition of past mistakes.

The voluntary conservation sector believe that conservation targets will not be achieved without a plan for action. Action or recovery plans should be produced for all priority species and habitats, should be soundly based on current scientific knowledge, and should specify both the conservation target and the actions thought necessary to achieve this target. Plans should at least contain:

- A brief analysis of threats;

- A statement of biological objectives;

- Broad policies;

- A plan for action.

The government has committed itself in the UK Action Plan to "complete and put into implementation plans for at least 90% of the presently known globally threatened and threatened endemic species within the next 10 years". The Government has made no commitment to produce habitat action plans, only to produce targets for key species.

Planning actions for habitats requires involvement from a wide range of organisations and individuals in order to meet objectives. For example, although the UK road building programme may not currently be specifically designed to damage UK biodiversity, this is currently one of its effects. Substantial changes are needed for a more environmentally sensitive policies on transport and energy. As another example, agricultural policy influences almost all aspects of UK biodiversity through direct and indirect impacts. Therefore it is vital that agricultural policies change to ensure biodiversity is conserved through environmentally sensitive land use systems. It is an important element of the Convention on Biological Diversity that Governments take a cross-sectoral approach to biodiversity. In the UK this means that biodiversity conservation is the responsibility of all Government departments not just the Department of the Environment.

6.7   Monitoring and review

Because of the inherent variability of animal and plant populations, and because of the demonstrated decline of those species targeted in *Biodiversity Challenge*, monitoring and review are vitally important parts of the process of maintaining biodiversity in the UK and reversing losses. Monitoring and review should be designed to answer the following questions:

• Are conservation targets being met?

• Are proposed actions still the right ones to meet targets for species and habitats?

• Have the priorities for action changed?

Monitoring and assessment must also review the effect of Government policies on biodiversity conservation. The review process must report on progress towards targets, refine or amend targets, assess the effectiveness of action taken, amend species and habitat action plans, and amend the generic summary of actions. *Biodiversity Challenge* suggests that the preparation of the Government's plan, *Biodiversity: the UK Action Plan*, should signal the beginning of a dynamic and growing process with the appropriate feedback loops.

6.8   Monitoring biodiversity

All species and habitats must be monitored sufficiently to establish whether or not they meet the quantitative criteria used in Red Data books or lists. *Biodiversity Challenge* sets out the priorities for biodiversity monitoring in the UK as:

- To establish and publish standard methods to monitor all species and habitats;

- Plan and implement monitoring programmes for invertebrates, mammals and lower plants as immediate high priorities;

- Agree a UK bird monitoring programme between the statutory agencies and the voluntary sector;

- Produce a 10 km square atlas of mammal distribution based on post-1990 data, by 1998 and implement the mammal 2000 monitoring programme;

- Monitor the effects on wildlife of acid deposition, nitrogen deposition, trophospheric ozone production and climate change;

- Monitor the effectiveness of management for species and habitats;

- Integrate monitoring of relevant land use processes with species and habitat monitoring.

6.9   Planning action for species and habitats

Biodiversity Challenge documents the main factors involved in protecting species, habitats and sites. Law enforcement and species legislation, covering persecution and collecting, together with recovery programmes, reintroduction and translocations are examples of methods or dedicated actions required to counter threats to individual species which cannot be conserved by actions directed at a habitat level.

The site safeguard method, which enables protection of species or habitats found in only a few locations, rather than being more widely distributed, is an important process which *Biodiversity Challenge* wishes to see strengthened. Sites are protected by a range of statutory designations such as SSSIs, Special Protection Areas (SPAs), Special Areas of Conservation (SACs), and Ramsar sites, together with national nature reserves, areas of special scientific interest and the legislative framework which supports their protection.

Biodiversity Challenge also considers the land use planning system, planning in the coastal and marine environment, indicative forestry strategies which describe the acceptability or otherwise of tree planting or afforestation in different zones, and factors operating at the forefront of agricultural policy. Important features of *Biodiversity Challenge* involve making biodiversity conservation one of the central objectives of common agricultural policy reforms, through reform in the arable sector and livestock sector, and to promote, across the whole countryside, that farmers and landowners should be given incentives to protect, manage and create habitats. *Biodiversity Challenge* also identifies that forestry policy requires clear ecological, economic and land-use objectives in order to contribute to biodiversity protection and enhancement, since many of our most important and rare habitats are threatened by afforestation including peatlands, heathlands and wet grasslands. To achieve this *Biodiversity Challenge* suggests a national forestry strategy which takes a long-term vision for forestry and its contribution to biodiversity by incorporating targets and timetables that are subject to monitoring and review. There should also be appropriate grant-aid to enable habitat creation and management in forestry for the benefit of wildlife. To this end there should be more open ground within forests, a higher proportion of broad-leaved trees in coniferous forests, more old trees and dead wood in forests, optimum age-class diversity in forests and minimal intervention wherever possible and appropriate.

Marine biodiversity is also a focus of the *Challenge* approach which states that the implications of modern fishing for marine ecosystems must be understood and acknowledged. A series of actions geared to removing the problems of over-fishing and environmental damage are proposed such as reducing fishing capacity, introducing a licensing system which establishes a transferable right to fish, managing the fisheries resource on a multi-species basis, tightly regulating industrial fisheries which threaten marine food chains, controlling the use of fishing gears and technologies such as beam trawlers, requiring a full environmental assessment for new fisheries, and minimising the incidental catch of undersized fish and other marine life.

In terms of water management, *Biodiversity Challenge* suggests that Government targets and mechanisms for water targets throughout the UK should include the production and implementation of catchment management plans for all UK catchments. These plans should contain a description of the impacts of agricultural practices on water quality and quantity, and promote increased integration of statutory bodies with responsibility for water management. There should be a statutory duty for all water management bodies to promote nature conservation and a statutory function for all water bodies to maintain and enhance the wetland biodiversity. To meet the objectives, consideration needs to be given to managing higher water levels, to ensuring no further loss of existing wetlands, and to restoring damaged wetlands by raising water levels.

7. BARRIERS TO IMPLEMENTATION

7.1 Lack of national/long-term datasets and future research needs

The Biodiversity Action Plan emphasises that action has to be based on information and understanding. Information should not just be narrowly taxonomic, but should contain information about distribution, habitat, ecology, life history, conservation status, abundance and key management requirements. There are significant gaps in these records which need to be filled. Past patterns of expenditure on research do not reflect planned investment of effort. It is now important to consider which are the most important subjects for study and research in the context of biodiversity conservation. In Chapter 1, it was suggested that the current distribution of effort results in neglect of less fashionable species, many of which may be more important in terms of ecosystem function. It may therefore be necessary to increase resources for conservation and research for the less charismatic species like lower plants, soil and other micro-organisms and invertebrates. It is simply not true that protection of one or two emblematic (or "indicator") species will guarantee the protection of everything else, because the ranges of other, associated species may be totally different. However, it is true that effective conservation actions have usually been based on studies of a few example species, rather than a study spread widely over many.

It is important to use resources where other support can lead to adequate results; this, in turn, interacts with popular interest. There is a limited number of data-sets which provide reasonably complete and uniform national coverage. There is an urgent need to maintain the continuity of the most extensive national datasets already in existence and also to explore the development of a more comprehensive national monitoring service. This may require further research into appropriate indicator or "example" groups which might form an appropriate basis for identifying targets and monitoring. Those data-sets which do currently provide national information on the "distribution and abundance of the biodiversity resource" tend to be unlinked, because they were often designed for other purposes and before the development of modern information technology allowed the potential for wider use.

"Sound science should underpin all environmental policy" (in the response by then science minister, William Waldegrave to a report on "Environmental Research Programmes" prepared by the Government's Advisory Committee on Science and Technology in 1992). However, the precautionary principle needs to be deployed, so that we do not delay action because of incomplete "proof".

Ecologists have been criticised for their reluctance at times to deploy incomplete knowledge. However, total knowledge is unachievable. In the words of the conservation scientist, M. Soulé, "The luxuries of confidence limits and certainty are ones that conservation biologists cannot now afford, given the rate of habitat destruction now documented. To embrace the purist's motto of "insufficient data" is to abandon the bleeding patient on the operating table". The Convention also notes "where there is a threat of significant reduction or loss of biodiversity, lack of full scientific certainty should not be used as a reason for postponing measures to avoid or minimise such a threat". The concept of "the basis of the best information currently available" is now well used and reasonably expected.

In ecological terms, some attempt has to be made to determine how biodiversity should be characterised and measured, so that the effectiveness of any conservation measures which are implemented can be measured, or evaluated. This begs questions relating to thresholds of viability, minimum viable population sizes, resilience and vulnerability to threat, re-creatability, the roles and times of density-dependence in population limitation, spatial dynamics of species and colonising potential.

Some of the key areas where further research would be useful are noted below. The requirements involve needs at various scales from local to international:

- What and where is our natural capital?;
- Targets (what do we want to achieve?)
  - — what is needed to contribute to national and international targets?
  - — what is needed in terms of local requirements and local people's aspirations?;
- The relationships between land-use policies and practices and species requirements;
- Minimum viable habitat sizes;
- Indicators of pollution/loss of viability;
- Understanding, definition and quantification of threats;
- Damage thresholds;
- Biodiversity hotspots;
- Natural areas/ biogeographic zones;
- Species and habitat requirements.

7.2   Lack of resources for conservation

An enlargement of the total base of protected areas is needed throughout the world. In the UK, a greater area is covered in roads than is included in SSSIs. The importance of those land-use practices which are sustainable and of benefit to wildlife needs better recognition. At present, policies such as those for agriculture tend to act against these by favouring intensification of food or forest production, even at times of food surpluses. Public payments should focus on the environmental benefits, common goods which do not have a market system.

Conservation policy well directed in one area may be counter-productive somewhere else. Measures must be carefully targeted to take account of regional variation. Blanket measures are unlikely to be effective; they need to be enabling rather than prescriptive.

From the European perspective, it is worth noting that there is no umbrella European plan corresponding to national plans of Member States. The Fifth European Environmental Action Plan is a version of a sustainability plan for individual countries, but it was written before Rio. The revised version ought to help to develop a European framework for progress towards sustainable development, but the signs are that it will be much more narrowly focused. This is important because nearly every action which could be undertaken by Member States to promote the conservation of biodiversity requires EU action to transform each one into concrete government commitments. At the present time, the most significant initiative at the European level which is intended to contribute towards meeting the requirements of the Convention, is the Habitats Directive, as well as the earlier Birds Directive. It is important to recognise that the Convention and the international obligations it engenders are not "hard law". The current attempts, using the Council of Europe, to develop a biodiversity and landscape strategy for Europe illustrate some of the difficulties. Some governments, notably the British, are reluctant to pursue this route even though they have already made more progress with their plan than many others. This is because such agreements are regarded by them as implying binding commitments. In contrast, many other governments see such approaches as targets to strive for, and as aids to progressive harmonisation of efforts between countries. Increases in mutual understanding and confidence are both requirements for, and potential benefits of, progress in this area.

This booklet has been concerned with the approaches to fulfilling the requirements of the Convention in the UK, and in a mainly European context. Lack of space has prevented consideration of the UK's impact abroad. However, in addition to such wider issues, the UK also has responsibility for international matters in a number of Dependent Territories. Many of them are islands rich in endemic life (Box 7.1) but are still not parties to major international treaty obligations. Further efforts are needed urgently, jointly with the people of these Dependent Territories, to promote conservation of biodiversity. Addressing these issues is a major outstanding priority.

Box 7.1. UK Dependent Territories and numbers of their endemic species: Information is sparse for certain groups of taxa and the numbers given are based on recorded endemics only.

Region Dependent Territory	Size (sq km)	Approx. human resident population	Numbers of endemic species of: Vascular plants	Terrestrial invertebrates	Reptiles and Amphibia	Birds *
Caribbean						
Anguilla	91	7000	1	-	-	-
British Virgin Islands	153	13000	unknown	1	5	0
Cayman Islands	263	18000	24	insects 38+	19	(16)
Montserrat	104	12000	2	6+	5	1
Turks & Caicos	500	7500	9	2+	8	-
Atlantic						
Ascension	97	1000	10	13	-	1
Bermuda	53	54700	14	1	-	1
British Antarctic Territory	1.7M	Uninhabited	-	a few	-	-
Falkland Islands	12173	1800	12	70% of all its insects	-	1(16)
St Helena	121	5600	46	ca. 300	-	1
South Georgia	3755	Uninhabited1	1	ca. 33% of all its insects	-	2
South Sandwich Islands	310	Uninhabited	-	unknown	-	-
Tristan da Cunha	169	313	40	60+	-	5(4)
Indian Ocean						
British Indian Ocean Territory	54400 (land area: 60)	Now uninhabited (except for naval base)	-	3	-	(1)
Pacific						
Hong Kong	1071	5400000	10	unknown	3	-
Pitcairn Islands	54	50	19	Henderson ca. 170	1?	2(2)
"Local"						
Gibraltar	6	29000	5	3	-	-
Guernsey	121	61700	-	-	-	-
Jersey	116	84100	-	-	-	-
Isle of Man	588	69800	-	-	-	-

* endemic subspecies are given in brackets
- signifies no endemic species known in this group in the Dependent Territory

8. MAJOR SOURCES AND FURTHER READING

Bignal, E.M., & McCracken, D.I., eds. 1992. *Prospects for nature conservation in European pastoral farming systems: a discussion document as an outcome of the Third European Forum on Nature Conservation and Pastoralism Ecology, 21-24 July 1992 University of Pau.* Joint Nature Conservation Committee, Peterborough.

Bignal, E.M., & McCracken, D.I. 1993. Nature conservation and pastoral farming in the British uplands. *British Wildlife,* **4**, 367-376.

Carter, I.C., Williams, J.M., Webb, A., & Tasker, M.L. 1993. *Seabird concentrations in the North Sea: an atlas of vulnerability to surface pollutants.* Joint Nature Conservation Committee, Peterborough.

Collis I and Tyldesley D 1993. *Natural assets: Non-Statutory Sites of Importance for Nature Conservation.* Local Government Nature Conservation Initiative.

Commission of the European Communities 1992. *Towards Sustainability, A European Community programme of policy and action in relation to the environment and sustainable development,* Commission of the European Communities, COM(92)23, 27 March 1992.

County Planning Officers' Society 1994. *Caring For Nature: A Guide to Good Practice in Nature Conservation.* CPO Society.

Department of the Environment 1987. *Circular 27/87 Nature Conservation.* HMSO. (Replaced during 1994 by *Planning Policy Guidance Note 9 on Nature Conservation).*

Department of the Environment 1993. *Environmental Appraisal of Development Plans: A Good Practice Guide.* HMSO, London.

English Nature 1993. *Position Statement on Sustainable Development.* English Nature, Peterborough.

Fuller, R.J. 1993. Farmland birds in trouble. *BTO News,* No. 184: 1.

Galbraith, C.A., & Bates, M. 1991. Regional forest strategies and bird conservation. In: *Britain's birds in 1989/90: the conservation and monitoring review,* ed. by D.A. Stroud & D. Glue. British Trust for Ornithology/Nature Conservancy Council, Thetford.

Haigh, N. 1994. *Manual of Environmental Policy: the EC and Britain,* Longman, Harlow.

Hampshire County Council (1994) *Hampshire County Council Structure Plan (Review): Nature Conservation*. Hampshire County Council.

Hill, D.A., Sotherton, N., Andrews, J. & Hawkins, J. 1995. Farmland. In: *Managing habitats for conservation*, ed. by W.J. Sutherland & D.A. Hill. Cambridge University Press, Cambridge.

Lindsay, R.A., Charman, D.J., Everingham, F., O'Reilly, R.M., Palmer, M.A., Rowell, T.A., & Stroud, D.A. 1988. *The Flow Country: the peatlands of Caithness and Sutherland*. Nature Conservancy Council, Peterborough.

NCC. 1984. *Nature conservation in Great Britain*. Nature Conservancy Council, Peterborough

Palmer, M. 1994. A UK *plant conservation strategy: a strategic framework for the conservation of the native flora of Great Britain and Northern Ireland*. Joint Nature Conservation Committee, Peterborough.

Pienkowski, M.W. ed. 1993. A contribution to the development of a system to assess nature conservation quality and to set targets for the national action plan required by the Convention on Biological Diversity. *JNCC Report No. 163)*, Joint Nature Conservation Committee, Peterborough.

Pienkowski, M.W., & Bignal, E.M. 1993. Objectives for nature conservation in European agriculture. In: *A future for Europe's farmed countryside*, ed. by J.B. Dixon, A.J. Stones & I.R. Hepburn, 21-43. (Proceedings of an international conference. Studies in European Agriculture and Environment Policy No. 1.) RSPB Sandy.

Pienkowski, M.W., Bignal, E.M., Galbraith, C.A., McCracken, D.I., Stillman, R.A. & Boobyer, M.G. 1995. A simplified classification of land-type zones to assist the integration of biodiversity objectives in land-use policies. *Biological Conservation*, **75**, 11-75.

Prendergast, J.R., Quinn, R.M., Lawton, J.H., Eversham, B.C. & Gibbons, D.W. 1993. Rare species, the coincidence of biodiversity hotspots and conservation strategies. *Nature,* **365**, 335-337.

Schemske, D.W., Husband, B.C., Ruckelhaus, M.H., Goodwillie, C., Parker, I.M. & Bishop, J.G. 1994. Evaluating approaches to the conservation of rare and endangered plants. *Ecology,* **75**, 584-606.

Stroud, D.A., Reed, T.M., Pienkowski, M.W., & Lindsay, R.A. 1987. *Birds, bogs and forestry. The peatlands of Caithness and Sutherland*. Nature Conservancy Council, Peterborough.

Stroud, D.A., Mudge, G.P., & Pienkowski, M.W. 1990. *Protecting internationally important bird sites: a review of the EEC Special Protection Area network in Great Britain*. Nature Conservancy Council, Peterborough

Tasker, M.L., Webb, A., Harrison, N.M. & Pienkowski, M.W. 1990. *Vulnerable concentrations of marine birds west of Britain*. Nature Conservancy Council, Peterborough.

UK Government 1994. *Biodiversity: the UK Action Plan, CM 2428*. HMSO, London.

UK Government 1994. *Biodiversity the UK Action Plan. Summary Report*. HMSO, London.

UK Government 1994. *Sustainable Development: the UK Strategy, CM 2426*. HMSO, London.

UK Government 1994. *Sustainable Forestry: the UK Programme, CM 2429*. HMSO, London.

UK Government 1994. *Climate Change: the UK Programme, CM 2427*. HMSO, London.

Wynne, G. ed. 1993. *Biodiversity challenge: an agenda for conservation action in the UK*. RSPB for the Biodiversity Challenge Group, Sandy.

Appendix1: Summary of the provisions of the Convention on Biological Diversity

The Convention on Biological Diversity signed by the UK Government in Rio on 5 June 1992 sets out a list of actions for governments to pursue in order to conserve biological diversity and to ensure the sustainable use of those species and habitats being exploited by man.

Of the 42 articles of the Convention, numbers 1-19 contain the most relevant parts in relation to scientifically based work on nature conservation. The needs relating to each of these relevant Articles is outlined below.

Article 1 states the objectives of the Convention, which are the conservation of biological diversity, the sustainable use of its components and the fair and equitable sharing of the benefits arising out of the utilisation of genetic resources.

Article 2 defines the terms used in the Convention. They include:

"Biological diversity" means the variability among living organisms from all sources including, *inter alia*, terrestrial, marine and other aquatic ecosystems and the ecological complexes of which they are part; this includes diversity within species, between species and of ecosystems.

"Biological resources" includes genetic resources, organisms or parts thereof, populations, or any other biotic component of ecosystems with actual or potential use or value for humanity.

"Sustainable use" means the use of components of biological diversity in a way and at a rate that does not lead to the long-term decline of biological diversity, thereby maintaining its potential to meet the needs and aspirations of present and future generations.

These terms are then used frequently throughout the following Articles.

Article 3 recognises the rights of signatory states to exploit resources within their country.

Article 4 states that the Convention will apply within national jurisdiction limits but that, for processes and activities, consideration beyond these boundaries may be required.

Article 5 strives for co-operation between states and between states and international organisations to help conserve biological diversity.

Article 6 outlines the need to construct national plans.

Paragraph 6a is a key part of the Convention in that it states that national strategies, plans or programmes for the conservation and sustainable use of biological diversity shall be developed. This may be achieved by adapting existing strategies, plans or programmes to meet the measures set out in the Convention.

Equally important, Paragraph 6b says that plans for the conservation of biological diversity and sustainable use must be integrated into other cross-sectoral plans.

Article 7 contains instructions for the elements of a national framework to identify and conserve biological diversity.

Paragraph 7a requires identification of components of biological diversity which are important for its conservation and sustainable use.

Paragraph 7b. These components must then be monitored through sampling and other techniques.

Paragraph 7c. Processes and categories of activities which have, or are likely to have, a significant adverse impact on the conservation and sustainable use of biological diversity should be identified. The effects of these factors should be monitored.

Paragraph 7d. Data derived from monitoring should be maintained and organised.

Article 8 This is a key Article in relation to conservation practice and is fundamental to the work of the statutory conservation agencies.

Paragraph 8a states that a system of protected areas should be established where special measures are taken to conserve biodiversity.

Paragraph 8b. Guidelines for the selection, establishment and management of these sites should be developed.

Paragraph 8c. Biological resources important for the conservation of biological diversity should be managed whether within or outside protected areas.

Paragraph 8d requires promotion of the protection of ecosystems, natural habitats and the maintenance of viable populations.

Paragraph 8e. Environmentally sound and sustainable development should be promoted in areas adjacent to protected areas.

Paragraph 8f. Degraded ecosystems should be restored and recovery plans for threatened species should be developed and implemented.

Paragraph 8g. Means should be established to regulate and control risks from release of genetically modified organisms.

Paragraph 8h. The introduction of alien species should be prevented, and alien species threatening natural systems should be controlled or eradicated.

Paragraphs 8i to 8m relate to developing the correct general conditions to allow conservation to take place, respecting local communities.

Article 9 encourages *ex situ* conservation where this is supportive to *in situ* measures.

Article 10 requires the integration of conservation and sustainable use of biological resources into national decision making, and that adverse impacts on biological diversity should be limited. Traditional cultures should be supported in practices compatible with sustainable use and to implement remedial action in degraded areas. Co-operation between government and the private sector should be encouraged to develop sustainable use.

Article 11. Economically and socially sound measures should be adopted to act as incentives for the conservation and sustainable use of components of biological diversity.

Article 12. Research and training, particularly for the special needs of developing countries, should be promoted contributing to the theme of the convention. A programme for scientific and technical training in aspects of the identification, conservation and sustainable use of biological diversity should be developed. Scientific co-operation should be enhanced.

Article 13 encourages measures to promote public education and awareness.

Article 14 requires impact assessments for proposed projects with a view to avoiding adverse effects.

Articles **15 and 16** relate to genetic resources and transfer of technology.

Articles **17, 18 and 19** promote exchange of information and technical and scientific co-operation.

The remaining Articles relate to the administration of the scheme and to other aspects not directly relevant to the present booklet.

Appendix 2: Addresses of contributors

David Baldock, Deputy Director, Institute for European Environmental Policy, 158 Buckingham Palace Road, London SW1W 9TR

Dr V Fleming, Scottish Natural Heritage. 2/5 Anderson Place, Edinburgh EH6 5NP

Dr David Hill, Ecoscope Applied Ecologists, Crake Holme, Muker, Richmond, North Yorkshire DL11 6QH; and 9 Bennell Court, Comberton, Cambridge CB3 7DS

David Pape, Planning Department, Hampshire County Council, The Castle, Winchester SO23 8UE

Dr M W Pienkowski, Director Life Sciences, Joint Nature Conservation Committee, Monkstone House, City Road, Peterborough PE1 4DG (present address: Head of International Legislation & Funding Department, Royal Society for the Protection of Birds, The Lodge, Sandy, Bedfordshire SG19 2DL)

Dr J Treweek, Institute of Terrestrial Ecology, Monks Wood, Abbots Ripton, Huntingdon, Cambridgeshire PE17 2LS

Mrs T Yates, Institute of Terrestrial Ecology, Monks Wood, Abbots Ripton, Huntingdon, Cambridgeshire PE17 2LS